Lucky Grandpa Had a Horse

Memories of a Danish Immigrant Family from Frederic W. Hansen Sr. Nina Strahan Hansen. Sophia Thomsen Hansen, and John G Thomsen.

Introduction and epilogue by
Robert J. Thomsen

Edited by
Robert J. Thomsen

*Cover photo is of Fred Hansen Sr. on his horse while in the United
States Army in World War I. Courtesy of Sharon Provines.*

Table of Contents

Introduction, by Robert J. Thomsen 1

The Hansen Family Tree.. 4

The Stories.. 6

Chapter 1 Hecla, South Dakota, by Fred Hansen.................................. 7

Chapter 2 Bird Island, Minnesota, by Fred Hansen 52

Chapter 3 Two Summers in Armstrong, Iowa, by Fred Hansen, Sr.................. 86

Chapter 4 Nina's Childhood Story, by Nina Strahan Hansen 112

Chapter 5 Sixty Years . . . and More, Part One, by Frederic W. Hansen, Sr. . 121

Chapter 6 Sixty Years . . . .. and More. Part Two, by Nina Strahan Hansen 148

Chapter 7 To My Children, by Sophia Hansen 156

Chapter 8 West-Fever, by John G Thomsen 164

Epilogue, by Robert J. Thomsen.. 186

Acknowledgements by Robert J. Thomsen...................................... 194

About the Author 195

Introduction, by

Robert J. Thomsen

Have you ever found an unexpected treasure? If so, you know how I felt when I first read the stories in this book. These words, simply told, opened for me vibrant glimpses of the lives of Danish immigrants in the Midwest United States in the late 19th and 20th centuries. Written by my father's first cousin, Fred Hansen, Fred's wife Nina, and his mother Sophia, they were originally written mainly for family with no expectations of a wider audience, but Fred indicates they were also written for the sheer joy of spinning a good yarn. Included, too, is an essay by Fred's cousin, John G Thomsen, about his experience as a second-generation Dane.

These stories begin with the tale of immigration common to so many Americans. The Hansen family was part of the great century of migration between 1820 and 1924 when fifty million people left Europe, thirty million of them bound for the United States. The Hansens were from Denmark and left for the same reasons that most of the 300,000 Danes left: greater economic opportunities. Those numbers, though, don't compare to the 1,116,000 Swedes or the 695,000 Norwegians, and in the bigger picture of 30,000,000 immigrants, Scandinavians are a very small percentage.1 Regardless of origin, a new immigrant arrived in an America where 7 percent of the population was made up of immigrants like themselves who were searching for ways to improve their lots in life.

What we hear next are intriguing details of heartbreak and courage in the frontier of the Dakota Territory when it was the edge of the American wilderness. In plain, straightforward language, Fred shares stories about family tragedies: deaths, failed crops, and a

---

[1] Hvidt, Kristian. *Danes Go West: A Book about the Emigration to America*. Copenhagen: Ribild National Park Society, Inc, 1976. p. 165.

devastating barn fire. We hear about life and work on a homestead: a homesick horse named Roy, a bank robbery, and a swindle in rural South Dakota, and finally about selling the farm near Hecla and moving the family and cattle by train to Minnesota.

In Chapter 2, Fred tells more about farming and family life in Bird Island, Minnesota: school and classmates, a mare named Bill, encounters with railroad-grading workers, a preacher's Model T, horse races at the county fair, and a hair-raising tale of murder. In Chapter 3, Fred relates experiences he had while becoming a veterinarian, mostly while visiting his Uncle John Thomsen in Armstrong, Iowa. In Chapter 4, we hear Fred's wife Nina reminisce about her childhood in Oklahoma, and in Chapter 5, Fred tells about his work as a veterinarian and life with Nina and their son Fred Jr. Then it's Nina's turn again as she picks up the story line in Chapter 6 and brings us to the time when these were written in the 1970's. Chapter 7 is a short, poignant reminiscence from Fred's mother, Sophia, reflecting on her childhood in Prussia-occupied Denmark and her immigrant experience. Finally, in Chapter 8 we have an essay written by Fred's cousin about his experience growing up as a second-generation Danish-American.

I came across these writings in our family papers when I was researching the life of my Danish grandfather (John Thomsen, the veterinarian uncle who Fred tells us about in Chapter 3), and I felt deeply that these stories need to be more widely known. Regardless of the country of origin, these immigrant stories connect us with the history of our country and give us identity as Americans. They tell about a time when the pace of life was slower. Rural electricity, telephones, and automobiles were not missed because they never had been and were scarcely imagined. Sixty miles an hour was an unthinkable speed, a man on the moon beyond imagination, and cell phones a fantasy.

We need this perspective; the frenetic pace of this 21st century seems only to increase. Like Alice in Wonderland, as our lives go faster so we must go faster just to keep up. Our only response to the constant barrage of new technology, new forms of communication, and new global challenges may become simple bewilderment. We need these stories so that we can step off the treadmill for a few moments and take a deep breath.

I was fortunate to find Fred's three granddaughters, my "Hansen cousins," in an internet search. When I proposed this project, they supported it at every step of the way with information, photos, and encouragement. Without them this project would not have happened. What a pity it would have been if these stories had continued to molder in boxes in our basements.

I hope, as did Fred, that you will enjoy these stories. I encourage you to use the family tree to sort out the characters; more information about them is In the Afterward, but you don't really need to keep them straight to enjoy the stories. Get a cup of hot cocoa, build a fire, and listen to story-tellers share a past we cannot live in any other way but through them.

The Hansen Family Tree

*Indicates children of the parents immediately above. **Bold** indicates that person appears again below.

Hans Jensen 1820-1881 & Marie Jensdatter 1821-1906

*Jens Peter Hansen 1883-?

*Hans Peter Hansen 1850-?

*Nils Peter Hansen 1852-?

*Lars Peter Hansen 1854-?

***Ole Peter Hansen 1857-1932**

*Frederick Hansen 1858-1888

*Jørgen (George) Hansen 1865-1888

Niels Thomsen Ganderup 1809-1896 & Christina Maria Johansen 1818-1901

Twelve children, including

*Niels Thomsen Ganderup (Niels Thomsen in USA) 1852-1928 & Christina Marie Rudebeck 1857-1928

    *John N. Thomsen 1884-1923

***Sophia Thomsen Ganderup** 1859-1943

*Jes Thomsen Ganderup (John Thomsen in USA) 1862-1923 &

Kirstine Thisgaard Thomsen 1888-1960

*John G Thomsen 1921-1998 & Pearle Johnson Maxwell 1920-2013

       *Three children including Robert J. Thomsen 1950-present

Ole Peter Hansen 1857-1932 & Sophia Thomsen Ganderup 1859-1943

*Olga S. Hansen 1890-1975

*George Hansen 1892-1918

*Frederic W. Hansen, Sr. 1895-1986 & Nina Strahan Hansen 1897-1996

>*Frederic W. Hansen, Jr. 1917-2001 & Florence Marie Logan Hansen 1919-2001

>>*Three Daughters born 1941, 1943, 1948

The Stories

All of the stories here are transcribed from manuscripts carefully typed by Fred Hansen, Sr. Editing has been for modern punctuation, paragraphing, and subject headings. Sophia used the Danish convention of capitalizing the first letter of the seasons and so did Fred; that usage is kept here. Also retained is Sophia's spelling of her native country, Danmark.

Chapter 1

Hecla, South Dakota, by Fred Hansen

Fred begins this story with his Grandma, Marie Jensdatter (1821-1906) and the circumstances of her immigration from Denmark to Greenville, Michigan, where her oldest son lived. She came with her husband, Hans Jensen, and the rest of her seven sons, including Fred's father, Ole. When Hans died in 1881, Ole and his mother along with his two younger brothers homesteaded in the eastern part of Dakota Territory. This is flat land, fertile when there is enough rain, near to the James River ("The Jim.") There they settled, even before the arrival of the railroad or the creation of the town of Hecla.

Fred goes on to tell how Ole met and married Sophia, and about his childhood on the homestead four miles south of Hecla, South Dakota. He paints vivid pictures of how tough it was to live on the frontier, deaths in the family, work on the farm, and tough decisions of how to survive. They learned, as did many, that the land, though fertile, could not support reliable crops without irrigation. They decided to pull stakes and move to Bird Island, Minnesota, about 200 miles to the east.

***

If this works out as it should, it will be a combination of family history, as it used to be told, and things I have remembered about people and happenings from my early years. Hopefully, it will be interesting enough so that parts will be retold to generations yet to come. Considering the great changes that have taken place in the way of life during my lifetime no one can predict what another century will bring. I believe, however, that no matter how great the changes are, children, as such, will be about the same. So do not be surprised if some youngster responds with something like,

"Grandma, that old grandpa you told about was pretty lucky. He had a horse."

Olga, George, and baby Fred with their Grandma, Marie Jensdatter Hansen. Hecla, South Dakota, about 1895.

Grandma—Marie Jensdatter Hansen

I can think of no one more fitting to start with than Grandma, who was my father's mother. She was a wonderful person who was gifted with an abundance of kindness, patience, and perseverance. She knew all the answers to the problems that confront small boys and had a way of her own of turning tears into smiles in almost no time at all. I know this to be true because she was an immediate member of our family until her death at the age of eighty-four years, at which time I was eleven. She had overcome most of the hurdles that had shown up in her path except the mastery of the English language. Because of this the family spoke Danish to her and when in her presence, and as a result my sister Olga, my brother George, and I all grew up with the ability to speak the language fluently. This has helped me many times and I am sure it has them as well. Although we sometimes used the Danish version of Bedstemor the name we commonly used was Grandma. I do not know why.

Grandma was born in 1822 in northern Denmark where life, at its best, was rugged. Her parents died when she was quite young and, as an orphan, she was 'bonded' to a farmer with whose family she lived and worked until she became of age. At about that time she married a young man who was then serving his term in the military service as was required by law. She soon learned that communication was necessary to a successful marriage but was handicapped by her inability to read or write since she had never attended school. She overcame this by getting a couple of elementary school books and, with the help of a friend, learning enough so that in a few weeks she could correspond with her husband. That satisfactory communication continued was evidenced by the family growing until there were seven sons.

Emigration from Denmark

Upon reaching the age of nineteen or twenty the oldest son sailed to America with his destination Greenville, Michigan, where friends had preceded him during the past couple of years. He wrote home that work was plentiful and the wages good so the parents prepared to follow by selling their belongings and arranging passage for themselves and the six boys as steerage passengers on a sailing ship for America and a whole new life. Grandma was forty-nine years old.

As steerage passengers in the hold of the ship, the trip, as they zig-zagged across the North Atlantic, was an experience that few would care to repeat. About a hundred people were assigned to a large, dimly lighted compartment which contained no furnishings except a huge table and a cook stove. Between their many trunks, chests, and bales there was just enough room for each person to spread blankets on the floor for sleeping. Turns were to be taken by families and groups for the use of the stove on which to prepare their food. When the weather was rough, as it was much of the time, the stove could not be used—for two strictly opposite reasons. First because of the danger of fire as the ship pitched and rolled, and second because, with the hatches battened down, there was not enough oxygen to support a fire. When candles could no longer burn, the hatches would be opened slightly to let in fresh air, which was often accompanied by cascades of cold water. The only toilet facilities were wooden buckets that were carried up two flights of stairs and emptied overboard, with the wind, if one was lucky. With someone seasick most of the time and vermin to contend with continually it was a long eight weeks before the ship arrived in New York. The immigrants were cleared through Ellis Island,[2] each one affixed with a tag giving name and address and loaded on the trains to take them to their many destinations. It must have been a welcome feeling for Grandma and her family to finally plant their feet on solid ground and to breathe in lungsful of clean pure air.

Greenville, Michigan

The father and older boys went to work at once in the logging woods. My father, who was fourteen, found a job as chore boy in a hotel and rooming house, and his two younger brothers started in school. For a few years the family prospered as they never had before. Then the older sons left home one by one to start lives and families of their own; the father, my grandfather, lost his life in a logging accident; and Grandma and her three remaining sons decided to find a way of life other than logs, saw mills, and grubbing out stumps.

Homesteading in Dakota Territory

My father, Ole P. Hansen, his mother Marie and his two younger brothers, Fred and George, learned that a part of Dakota Territory was being opened for homesteading and came west, lured by the

---

[2] Actually, Castle Clinton in New York, the predecessor of Ellis Island, which didn't open until January 1, 1892.

promise of free land. They settled in Brown County, which later became a part of South Dakota. In contrast to the area in Michigan from which they came, where lumber dominated every activity, this was open prairie with about the only trees being a few clumps of willows along the river and an occasional cottonwood, which served as a landmark more than anything else.

The end of the railroad was at Columbia, but since the land nearby was already taken, the three men filed on claims about twenty miles north. This meant that all supplies, including lumber, groceries, coal for winter heating and summer cooking, and everything else had to be hauled that distance either by horses or ox teams. The railroad did, however, keep moving north and after a few years a town, Houghton, came into being seven miles south of Father's place, and later Hecla was established, five miles north. Hecla became the post office and trading center for the family. Aberdeen, the county seat, was thirty-five miles south of Hecla.

Farming for the first, or pioneer years, was difficult and very unsuccessful. Drought ruined many of the crops and the distance from market was a handicap. Since this was former buffalo country, as indicated by the hundreds of bleached skeletons from the hide hunting days of twenty or so years before, Father reasoned it should be a good place to raise livestock. So at every opportunity he increased his cattle herd by buying, often at a bargain, the animals of homesteaders who were ready to give up and leave. On this basis he probably did not prosper but did manage to hold his own against the prairie and the elements.

Ole Meets Sophia

After six or seven years in Dakota, Father decided to take a trip back to Denmark—this time with a second-class ticket instead of steerage. Although he denied this, it was said the purpose of his visit was to find a wife to help him make a home. Anyway, he stopped for a few days to visit a cousin in Chicago and while there met a young Danish woman who was a seamstress and dress maker. They were interested in each other and he said he would stop again on his way home. The people and places in Denmark were not as interesting as he thought they would be so he cut his visit short. This time in Chicago he and the dressmaker, whose name was Sophia Thomsen, became engaged. She promised to come to Dakota the following summer and arrived at Columbia on her twenty-sixth birthday, June 27th, 1887. They were married the same day.

Sophia Thomsen Ganderup

The district in Southern Denmark where Mother was born had been a point of dispute between Denmark and Germany for many generations. At times troops were stationed there, both to maintain order and to prevent a sudden military takeover. If Danish soldiers were not available, mercenaries from other countries were often hired. A company of Spanish soldiers were quartered in an old castle in the village along about the years of 1805 or 1806. The building caught fire and burned, making it necessary to move the Spaniards to another location. One of them was ill and unable to travel so was left in the care of the village clockmaker and his family. When he regained his health, he began to learn the trade from his benefactor, married one of the daughters and, with the passage of time, became the village clockmaker himself. He was my great-grandfather.[3] He and his father-in-law had a part in making the old grandfather's clock that Fred and Florence now have in their living room in Springfield, Virginia.

---

[3] We in the John G Thomsen family have always doubted this story. However, I am now a true believer. This man was my great-great grandfather. Recent genetic testing determined that I am about 2.6% Bedouin. That could quite plausibly have come from this man. RJT

Map of upper Midwest.

When Mother was only three years old, the territorial dispute was ended by Germany gaining the annexation. (Incidentally the area was returned to Denmark in 1920.) This transfer to German control gave her the advantage of learning the Danish traditions and language as well as being made to follow the strict discipline and requirements of German educational rules. Her basic schooling was much better than that of most immigrants of that period.

Mother was the youngest daughter of eleven children. Of these, five migrated to America. They did not come in a group as did Father's family but made the trip one by one over a period of years. The first brother left home when she was a very small child. He was an adventurous sort and not given much to correspondence. The last, and one of the few notes received from him, told that he was a trooper in the Seventh U.S. Cavalry and stationed in the northwest part of Dakota Territory.[4] From the date it was later found that this was shortly before the Battle of the Little Big Horn. It is assumed that he was killed there. Of the others, a sister became a housewife in Chicago, a brother established a shoe store in Clinton, Iowa,[5] and the other brother attended and graduated from the Toronto Veterinary College, established a practice at Armstrong, Iowa and became one of the state's outstanding veterinarians. He was my Uncle John, of whom the family has all heard.[6]

The family with whom Mother traveled from Denmark had as their destination Detroit, Michigan. She stayed with them for a while and then went to Clinton, Iowa, where her brother Niels was settled. While there she worked at housework until she became familiar enough with the language to feel at ease among strangers. With this accomplished she proceeded to Chicago to make her way as a dressmaker, an art or trade at which she was adept. This ended, as has been told before, with her marriage and the role of pioneer in the Dakota Territory.

Family Tragedy—1888

The year following Father's and Mother's marriage they and Grandma suffered two severe and shocking blows with the deaths of his two younger brothers, Fred and George. The former succumbed to an illness and the latter was struck by a bolt of lightning. Fred was married and lived a few miles away, but Father's and George's land adjoined and they had operated somewhat together, making adjustments necessary.

---

[4] We have been unable to verify this part of the story. No Ganderup or Thomsen is listed in the US Army casualties at the Little Big Horn. RJT
[5] Niels Thomsen.
[6] Much more on him in the chapter on Armstrong Stories.

Hard Times in Grain Farming

For a couple of years there had been a reasonable amount of rain, and some fairly good crops were harvested in the neighborhood. With the railroad building north, and Houghton already going as a town, Father decided to try grain farming again. The result was disastrous. For five successive years there was not enough grain harvested to replace the seed. During this time, however, Mother learned to drive horses and to operate the different kinds of farm machinery and so was able to take the place of a man in the fields. She continued this even after the first two children were born, with Grandma taking care of the house and the children. By then Father was through with raising grain, except for that needed for the livestock, and again began to build up his cattle herd.

The Hansen Family in Hecla, South Dakota around 1900 – left to right – Olga, Ole, Fred Sr., Sophia, George

Father and Mother both had the same background of poverty and the same goal of financial independence. This, they decided, would require more land and livestock. So with neighbors giving up in discouragement and moving away, they bought and went deeper in debt whenever they could raise or borrow money. They both have said that if they had had a place to go they might have followed the neighbors who left. But it worked out pretty well this way.

Farm Expansion and Galloway Cattle

By the time I was old enough to begin remembering things the worst of the "hard times" were over. Father and Mother were very much in debt, probably more than ever, but their affairs had taken on a semblance of stability with prosperity not too far away. They were still buying land and continued to do so for several years yet until they owned over two thousand acres of pasture and hay land, with leases on still more. Father was a good judge of values and a fair bargainer but was inclined to follow the theory that if a little was good, more was better. Mother was more conservative and acted as a kind of damper on his activities. He had become experienced in the handling of livestock and realized that cattle of good quality could be raised as easily and more profitably than those that were inferior. When given a chance to buy a registered Galloway bull and twenty cows, he did not hesitate to stretch his credit to the limit and do so. From these he developed one of the outstanding Galloway herds in the state, was given honorable mention in the herd books of the breed, built up sales of breeding stock, and twice—once at the stockyards in Chicago and again at Sioux City—topped the market for the day in carload lots. He was proud of Hansen's Galloways, and justifiably so.

Religion

I think Olga, George, and I were fortunate in having the parents we had. They were honest and industrious and, even though they did at times seem overly strict, they were just and fair and their decisions were for our betterment. They belonged to and supported the

Lutheran Church at Houghton but did not wear religion on their sleeves. There was always a Bible on the table in the "Sitting Room" but I do not ever remember it being read as a ritual. Neither was the practice of asking Grace at meals ever followed.

Mother was zealously opposed to the use of alcohol in any form and was active all her life in the W.T.C.U.[7] In the knowledge that the Methodist Church had a background of Prohibitionism she felt more at home with this group in Hecla than with the Lutherans in Houghton.[8] We attended both Church and Sunday school in Hecla off and on but had no pattern. I am sure the folks were Christians but missing a day of school during the week seemed a greater sin than missing church.

Grandma was the most faithful member of the family as far as religion was concerned and took much comfort from her Danish Bible and Testament.

Work on the Farm

At a time when a youngster who could ride a horse or drive a team could often take the place of a grown man, it is not surprising that hard working parents found plenty of things for us children to do. Although at times the days seemed unending and the work over tiring, I did not then, nor have I since, resented the custom that was followed. It was accepted as the way of life; the children on neighboring farms worked the same way and it was, without question, good training. We were given credit for doing our part in the family enterprise, we did have time for play, and often were treated to highly compensating pleasures.

Outings from the Farm

---

[7] The WTCU was the Woman's Christian Temperance Union, established in 1873.

[8] Despite this the family burial plot is at the Lutheran Church in Houghton.

The outstanding one of these was the annual trip—usually in June—to the circus in Aberdeen. A couple of weeks of anticipation preceded the event. On the designated day, Father, Mother, Olga, George, and I would leave home about four o'clock in the morning for the thirty some mile drive to Aberdeen. Grandma never cared to go and said our report would please her as much as seeing the sights. Mother always packed a picnic lunch, and with ice cream, candy and fruit, fresh from the store, we did not lack for food. It would be after eight by the time the horses were stabled and fed and we were along Main Street waiting for the parade. Father was well acquainted at the Court House and the bank and could often find us a place of vantage from which to watch. Following this, things happened so fast that it was difficult to remember which was first in our report to Grandma. The sight of all the animals, the many acrobatic and clown acts in the circus rings, and the rides on the merry-go-round were such that it was almost impossible to keep a clear head and stay awake on the way home.

Another outing that we had each summer was a Sunday picnic at Tacoma Park. This was on the bank of the James River and about twenty miles from home. The grownups would visit and the children would find some kind of a game to play, and Father always rented a row boat and took us for a ride on the river. We would come home not as tired as from the circus but with the feeling of a pretty good day.

Then there were church picnics in a grove about a mile from home and always the Fourth of July in Hecla. With visiting neighbors on Sundays and neighbors visiting us, and the games we played among the three of us, together with a good supply of books and a few toys, we did not really suffer for lack of recreation.

More Work on the Farm

For several of my younger years, and until an addition was built on the house, George and I slept together. In the mornings Father would say, "George, it is time to bring in the horses." It seemed he never would get through jiggling the bed while he dressed but finally he would leave and I could enjoy the luxury of another hour's sleep. George was a persuasive sort and began telling me of the thrill of being out right after daybreak and whooping and hollering all over the pasture and seeing those horses head for home at a dead gallop. I went with him for a couple of times but did not get too much of a thrill. He said he was sure it would grow on me and after another day or two suggested that I go out by myself while he found some other chores to do. I did these two or three times, and then Father's morning call changed to, "George" a pause and then, "Fred, it is time to bring in the horses."

Hired Man

About this time we had a man from the Finnish settlement north of Hecla hired by the day to help in haying. His name was Sylvester Kite—shortened from Kitoinen. He was not much account, but he did have a bearing on my future work days. He slept in the hay mow of the barn as was customary on farms with small houses. One Sunday he came home with a bottle and a cardboard box. He made frequent trips to the barn to nip at his bottle and kept telling us kids that he had something in the box that would scare the daylights out of us as soon as it became dark. When it finally did, he lit a lantern and hung a "dancing skeleton," made from cardboard and rubber bands, in the doorway and accompanied with contortions with weird, high pitched Finnish songs. It soon became bedtime, and shortly after, he came to the kitchen door with a blanket on his arm to ask if he might sleep on the floor since he had scared himself so that he dared not go to sleep in the barn. A week later he came back with a watch. Father had the faculty of telling time by the sun, or without it, with a high degree of accuracy, but the next day Sylvester named the quitting time and rather than argue with a watch they came home an hour early. The next morning Father took enough money along to pay him off if yesterday's incident was repeated.

When Sylvester again announced quitting time, he told him to take his watch and get going and to be sure he was off the place when he got home. With the end of Sylvester, George was advanced to operate the stacker. I drove the team on the bucker and became a full-fledged member of the haying crew.

Aberdeen

From time to time, Father had business trips to make to Aberdeen. These mostly had to do with real estate sales, titles, and taxes and notes due or loans to be made at the bank. Mother sometimes went with him, when both their signatures were necessary on a document, and at others he often took one of us children, providing it did not interfere with school. My first of these trips, before I was old enough to be in school, was probably the most impressive. We went by train which by itself was quite a thrill. The highlight of the day was the climb up the spiral staircase in the exact center of the courthouse to the observation platform at the dome. This was maybe three stories high and I am sure the people and horses below did not look as small as my imagination made them seem. It was high enough, though, that it was natural to grasp the railing firmly with one hand and to hold onto Father with the other, just in case something happened. Next, after the stop at the bank, was dinner at the Sherman House which was Aberdeen's biggest hotel. Before eating we washed in the rest room where there were faucets with hot and cold running water and chains to pull on flush toilets—contraptions that had not yet made their way to Hecla. After dinner we bought presents to take home in the form of a handkerchief for each one. The last stop before taking the horse drawn bus from the Sherman House to the depot was at Martin's store. Miss Martin was the school teacher who roomed at our place and whose father owned the store in Aberdeen. She had written a note to him and asked me to deliver it. I do not know what she wrote but he gave me a sack of candy in return. Although I was tired when we got home it was an outing to be remembered.

State Capital

South Dakota became a state in 1889 but ten years later no decision had been made as to which of the two competing towns—Pierre or Mitchell—would be chosen as the Capital. The Milwaukee railroad favored Mitchell and the Northwestern backed the campaign for Pierre. They both advertised free rides to everyone to come and see their favorite city. Mother took Olga and George to Mitchell and a week or so later Father took me to Pierre. The closer we got the more crowded the train became until it was impossible for the conductor to make his way through the aisles.

When we arrived, the town itself was just as crowded. There were several friends from Hecla who stayed pretty much together. I remember seeing Indians with feathers, buffalo, and cowboys riding bucking broncos up and down the street and scattering the people right and left. There were souvenir stands and carnival games everywhere.

Sleeping rooms were out of the question since any place with a bed had been reserved long in advance. There was a tent where blankets and cots were for rent but it did not appear too inviting and the attendants did not seem too trustworthy so Father and some of his acquaintances from Hecla found room in a private home where we were given blankets and a pillow and all of us slept on the rag-carpeted floor of the sitting room. Eating was a kind of fun though with meals eaten on plank tables in a large tent. Everyone lined up and as each one paid his way, he was handed a tin plate, a cup, and a fork, knife and spoon. The food was good and after eating, the tableware was dropped in tubs with a clatter. I think everyone was relieved when train time came and they knew the end of the excursion was in sight. At the depot we were bid farewell by the Salvation Army band which also had been the first group to welcome us when we arrived.

An incident occurred in connection with this which was amusing to most of the passengers except one. It was beyond my understanding, at the time, but was retold so many times in later years that I shall include it here. The banker from Hecla was known for his extreme stinginess and was perhaps the most unpopular individual in our group. After boarding the train, he discovered he had dropped a five dollar gold piece on the Salvation Army tambourine instead of the penny he had intended. He bemoaned his bad luck all the way home and ignored all the free advice that was offered. Fortunately, Father found a seat and I either sat on his lap or stood between his knees and slept until we arrived at Hecla. There were hardy individuals who boasted of visiting both Mitchell and Pierre two and three times but once was enough for most.

School Board Money

Father and Mother were very much opposed to gambling, although their way of life was a game of chance and some of their transactions might have been of credit to a poker player. As treasurer of the school board, Father kept the school funds in his personal checking account. This was legal and convenient.

One spring he had a chance to buy a small bunch of cattle at a bargain price and, since his own funds were inadequate, decided to borrow the money from the school. This was not much of a gamble since he would have livestock to ship to market long before there would be bills to pay for the school. A friend of Father's told him that at the coming annual meeting of the school board someone was going to ask where the funds were deposited since his bank account was too low to include them. The day of the meeting Father visited another good friend, Pete Wolf, a well-to-do bachelor who lived ten miles east and borrowed, in cash, the exact amount of the school account.

The meeting proceeded without a hitch until near the end when one individual arose and said he had checked at the bank and learned the school money was not on deposit there and he, and a few others, would like to know where it was. Father replied that he had little confidence in a bank where anyone could walk in and find the amount in another man's account; he had withdrawn the money and had in his pocket the exact amount shown in his treasurer's report. With that he placed a fat and bulging billfold on the desk and invited anyone to count it who chose to do so. No one did. He continued that, as soon as possible, he would open an account at a bank in Aberdeen where the officials would not be as free with their information. The dissenters knew they had been taken in some way, but did not quite know how. Before going to bed, Father rode over and returned the loan to Pete Wolf. But he would not gamble.

Sophia's Teeth

It seems Mother was well able to keep things to herself too. In her early twenties, when she first began earning money, all her teeth had been pulled and she had been fitted with dentures. They were about the best set of false teeth anyone could wish for. She could eat corn, raw apples, and carrots without trouble as well as snip threads in her needle work. They fit her so well that she and Father were married well over two years before he learned that they were not real. The way he found out made a good story in later years but at the time it must have been quite a shock. Sometime before Olga was born Mother became ill and dizzy while washing clothes. Father caught her as she swayed. Then, as she fainted and became utterly relaxed, her mouth opened and her teeth—both uppers and lowers— came slithering out. Father called, "Oh My God." Since he was a man who was never known to swear, it is believed his words were intended as a supplication rather than as an expletive.

Peddlers

There was an unwritten rule that anyone coming to the house near mealtime must be invited in and, if towards evening, a stranger would be offered lodging for the night. This might mean sleeping in the hay mow or on the kitchen floor but, at any rate, it was shelter.

Pay was seldom offered and never accepted. Strangers, if they stayed overnight, might try to help with chores, and peddlers, who came a time or two each summer, insisted on leaving a gift from their wares with the women of the house.

The peddlers were a class of people all to themselves They were all dark-complected and said to come from southern Europe or some far off place referred to as the Balkan States. They were fairly young men and strong enough to carry their heavy packs day after day in all kinds of weather. They appeared to know very little of the English language, but there were some who said this was just a pretense in order to give them an edge in bargaining.

At our house Grandma was their best customer. She loved to buy combs and was always ready to dicker for a new pair of glasses. There might have been optometrists and ophthalmologists in the cities but most people then bought their glasses over the counter by trial and error method. So it was a treat for Grandma to have a display delivered right into the kitchen. After trying several pairs and deciding which seemed the best, the trading would begin. The peddler would name a price which seemed much too high and Grandma would make an offer so low that of course he could not accept it. With broken English on both sides and gestures and facial expressions that were more eloquent than words, they might come within twenty-five cents of a price that would be agreeable to both. Neither one would budge. Grandma would turn to her kitchen work as if the peddler did not exist. He would repack his valise and start for the door. About then, as a rule, one or both would reconsider and give a little and Grandma would have her new glasses. She would then treat him to a cup of coffee and a snack and they would part as friends—he apparently pleased with making a sale and she with the satisfaction of having driven a hard bargain.

There were also peddlers of Watkin's and McConnell's remedies and spices and flavorings but they were local people who followed regular routes and traveled with teams and buggies.

Mother usually dealt with them and looked forward to their coming.

Bank Heist in Hecla

When George was quite small he fell one evening, while playing on some old boards, and ran a rusty nail through the palm of his hand. Grandma applied carbolic acid and sweet oil to the injury and used packs and poultices, but his hand continued to swell and become more painful by the hour. About midnight Father hitched a horse to the two-wheeled cart and took George for a fast ride to see the doctor in Hecla. The town seemed deserted as he drove down Main Street but as he tied the horse to a hitch rail, a man with a gun stepped out of the shadows and, in a low voice, told him to get back in the cart and leave town. Father showed him George's hand and explained that he wanted only to see the doctor. The gunman, with threats, insisted that he get going and come back at daylight. Father was scared of the man and the gun but was more afraid of blood poison and stood his ground until the stranger relented but made him promise he would not say a word to the doctor or anyone about this meeting and would leave for home as quickly and quietly as possible. The doctor treated George's hand, sent home medicine to dress it with enough laudanum[9] to keep him groggy for a couple of days, and he recovered without further incident. Father was not greatly surprised when he heard the next day that robbers had blown open the safe and robbed the bank shortly after he left for home.

Several years later I sometimes spent a night in town with a friend of my age, Durward Ferris, who with his parents lived in the apartment over the bank. Once Mr. Ferris folded back a rug and showed us a trap door that had been built in the floor above the safe right after the robbery[10]. As far as I know there was never an occasion to use it.

---

[9] Tincture of Opium.
[10] The trap door presumably was a safety escape route in case someone was locked inside the vault.

Olga and Prince

This happened long before my time but the story was told so often that I shall repeat it. When Olga was two or three years old, Father one day was trying to break a wild young horse that had never been haltered or handled before. He managed to get a harness on the animal but in the process the horse had kicked down part of his stall and a hole in the wall of the barn and, as Father left to get a hammer and nails to patch up some of the wreckage, it continued to strike and kick at anything that moved. When he returned, he was pleased to hear that the commotion had eased but then, to his dismay, he discovered that Olga was standing and stroking the horse's hind leg and saying, "Nice Prince." It must have been a great relief when she came to him when he called.

Cattle and Hay

As children we had little to do with the field work connected with the Spring plowing and seeding since this was taken care of before the school term was over. Our morning and evening chores increased with the season and we might be called upon to take a place in the field on a Saturday but our actual work began with helping to sort and move the cattle to the assigned pastures, of which there were four. Two of these, one of which was leased, were a mile east of our buildings and were side by side with a road separating them. Each was a section of land. A section means that each was a mile square and each contained 640 acres. Both had windmills, on short towers, that were set on gear[11] when the cattle were moved in and were allowed to run day and night until the herd was removed later in the season.

For the first few weeks, until the animals settled down in their new surroundings, it was necessary to check and check these pastures two or three times a week. This meant counting the

---

[11] The gear engaged the windmill rotor to the pump. If the gear was not engaged the windmill still spun but the pump did not pump water.

numbers, oiling the windmills, distributing salt, and riding slowly around inside of each of the four miles of fence and looking for missing staples, broken wires, and weakened posts. The first time around was fun but as the weeks drew on the fences seemed longer, the saddles became harder and hotter, and it even felt as if the horses were trying to walk as stiff legged as possible. We began then to look forward to haying, which was the most important work of the year but also the hardest and most tiring.

Haying started right after the Fourth of July and the crew consisted of Father, Olga, George, and myself. As a rule, Olga and I would each run a mower for two days while Father and George moved the stacker and bucker to the field. Then George would rake most of the second day and we were ready to stack. If the crop was fairly good Olga could pretty well keep ahead of the stacker with the mower and rake.

The stacker was a large framework of uprights, arms, ropes, and pulleys with a fork that was capable of lifting a half ton of hay at a time and dropping it on the stack. The bucker, which I ran, was an implement about fourteen feet wide with a horse hitched at either side. Between the horses were twelve, eight foot, metal tipped wooden tines. As I would drive, with one horse on each side of a freshly raked windrow, the tines would slide under the hay until it often piled so high I had to stand on the seat in order to see where to go. This load would be pushed onto the stacker fork, the horses backed away, and George, after trimming up the loose ends, would start the stacker team and deliver the load to father who would arrange it and shape the stack.

Most of the hayfields were a mile or two from home so we took feed and a barrel of water for the horses and our own noon lunch. The horses were fed in the wagon box and the four of us ate in the shade underneath. We were hungry enough by noon so we did not pay much attention to the dust the horses made when stamping flies or the occasional kernel of oats that had to be picked from a sandwich or dish of potato salad.

I do not know how Mother could prepare and pack such tasty, and apparently wholesome, meals day after day with no thought and little knowledge of refrigeration any more than I can understand how one man and three children, teenagers and less, could put up enough hay in one season to carry between two and three hundred head of cattle through a Dakota winter.

Roy

Father raised quite a few horses which Olga, George, and I knew would sooner or later be sold. We accepted this as a fact of life until one of our favorite animals became the victim. We would then pout, sulk, give short answers, and make disparaging remarks for a few days and then return to normal. During those days we must have been a miserable trio to live with. Once in a while—I shall change that to once, at least—such an incident had a storybook ending.

It began when we came home from school and found that Roy had been sold. We immediately began our act and missed few chances to interpose remarks such as that Roy was one of the best horses we ever had; maybe the new owner would beat him around the head with a club; we probably would not get much hay put up this year with all the best horses sold; maybe Roy would be tied outside of the saloon for hours on end while the owner was inside drinking whiskey, and it could not do much good to go to school to try to amount to something if somebody was always selling the good horses while we were away.

The last two remarks were our powerhouse and about as far as we dared to go. Then one afternoon, when we had found that life was livable without this particular animal, a team came down the road with a gaunt and dejected Roy tied behind the wagon. The buyer said he was bringing him back because he was sick and would not eat, drink, or mix with other horses. Father said he could have his choice of another horse or the return of his money. Roy was led into the barnyard but seemed to be in a daze with no idea of where he was. He looked sick without any question.

After a minute or so he lifted his head a little, saw the water tank and took a hesitating step or two towards it when suddenly he realized he was home. He plunged his mouth in the water and drank until it seemed he would burst. He then put his nose in deep and snorted a time or two, backed away, and lay down and rolled over and over in the dirt. Then with his mane and tail flying he ran at full gallop to the pasture and the horses he knew. The buyer said, "I'll be damned. That was the home-sickest horse I ever saw." Whether he took another animal or his money I do not remember, but the main thing was we had Roy back.

Olga and Baby Fred

The story was often told about Olga, when she was five years old, awakening one night and sensing that something unusual was taking place. She went to Grandma's bed, in the same room, to ask about it but found that it was empty. Lights were showing from the kitchen and Father's and Mother's room so she started that way, arriving just in time to see the doctor pick up a brand-new baby and slap him twice right where it hurt the most. She promptly expressed her feeling about that sort of treatment and, by virtue of discovery, laid claim to the newcomer and the responsibility for his well-being from then on. Of course, I was too small at that time to know all this but it was not long before I realized she was my Guardian Angel and Knight in Shining Armor all in one. This bond held through childhood, through adult life, and continues through the years. It is a pleasant thought to reflect upon.

During my first years at country school Olga was always there to take my part, to encourage me when discouraged and to enlarge upon any special credit I might occasionally earn. In looking back, I am sure my problems were actually few. They were divided into the ones to be taken to Grandma or Father and Mother, and to Olga

29

or George.

Olga Hansen taken in Aberdeen, South Dakota. This is probably her graduation photo. Dress was Sophia's wedding dress.

Bob Mitchell

Olga would come to my aid promptly and without question, while George would study the situation before committing himself. One such instance had to do with giving Bob Mitchell a good beating and, of course, I could not ask Olga to do that. Bob and I were good friends. He was my senior by a year, outweighed me by twenty pounds and was much tougher by having five older brothers to contend with. One day he was hitting me on the muscles of the arms with his fist, which was quite painful, but when I tried to fight back he outclassed me in every way.

This went on for several days so I asked George to pitch in and help me. After thinking about it for a while he explained that it would not work and would only be an invitation for his many brothers to get into the fight, too. He would, however, teach me to fight and train me over the weekend so that I would be more than a match for Bob. To do this he tied the leg of a pair of pants to make a sack, filled it with oats and hung it up so as to serve as a punching bag. I was to swing at this as hard and fast as I could with my clenched fists during the next couple of days and since surprise was very important, I was to practice walking unconcernedly by and then suddenly turning to attack.

By Monday morning I was both trained and tense. As we entered the school yard George took my lunch pail and I walked on, ready for whatever came and trying to assume a nonchalant attitude. Suddenly I saw Bob's lips move and will never know if he said a dirty word, gave me a friendly smile, or was speaking to someone else. From a standing start of four feet away I started with fists flying. He dodged, which the oats sack had not done, but my momentum stood me in good stead and the top of my head hit him on the jaw and down he went with me on top and swinging at any part that moved. When the damage was assessed, he had a badly cut lip, a bleeding tongue, and a black eye that lasted for days. The teacher kept us both after school and made us copy some adage on the blackboard many times. Then we had to shake hands before she let us go. This was not necessary since we were friends anyway. We walked home together, plotting ways to get even with the teacher.

High School

There was not yet a high school in Hecla when Olga finished the eighth grade, so she continued her schooling by attending the Normal School in Aberdeen for the next two or three years. It was a great treat when she could come home for an occasional weekend or holiday. To keep her posted I tried to write to her and tell the news, which amounted to which mare had a new colt and the horses that were being broken and which I would choose for her haying team

31

next summer.

Then George finished country school and also went to Aberdeen for a year, when finally the high school in Hecla opened and the three of us made the daily trip of five miles each way, five days a week. In the short winter days, we would leave home before daylight in the mornings and get home again after dark, with the temperature often 25 to 35 degrees below zero. I remember being wedged in the seat between Olga and George all wrapped in robes and blankets. With a big sister on one side and a fair-sized brother on the other and a team that knew the way home and was anxious to get there, I was snug and secure.

Olga was a member of the first graduation class of the Hecla High School. The next year she entered the University of Minnesota to study Medicine. She was able to make only one visit home that winter and, of course, we all missed her a great deal. George and I continued school in Hecla. He was in his second year of high school and I finished the eighth grade. That turned out to be our last year in Dakota.

Hecla Watch Repair

Hecla was a busy little town but it did lack a few businesses, one of which was a jewelry store and watch repair service. Then, when I was about ten years old, a watch repair man named Z.P. Barber came to town and rented room in Tyson's general store. The local paper—*The Hecla Standard*—carried his advertisement and introduced him in a column as well qualified and anxious to open a full-fledged jewelry store if this introductory enterprise was a success.

Father had an old watch in a huge gold hunting case that I had always admired and had often played with when I was smaller. He told me if I wanted to take it in and have it fixed, I could have it, but said plainly to learn the cost of the repair in advance and, under no circumstances, to leave it if the charge was to be over three dollars and a half. If it was more than that he would go himself and try to make a deal. Even with that restriction I was walking almost on air when I went to see Mr. Barber. There was no doubt that he knew his business. It took him a very short time to learn the limit of my finances and much less to find the repairs would come to exactly three dollars and fifty cents.

The job took much longer than I had expected. Every time any of us went to town the report was the same. He had had to send for a part and he was very busy. This was evident by the great number of watches he had hung on hooks on a pine board by his work table. Finally, after about four weeks, it was ready. I paid the bill and was told the watch was in fine shape and was keeping perfect time. It might be, though, that body movement would affect it some and if so, he could correct it easily. By the next day it had lost three hours so I took it back. Mr. Barber explained that he was terribly busy but wanted, above all else, to adjust my watch to perfection, so to plan to leave it with him at least a week. The next seven days were long and by then the trip to town had to be postponed a couple of days for some reason.

When I finally did get there, I was stunned by the unbelievable news that Z.P. Barber had left town with my watch and a hundred more of others and the money he had collected for repairing them. In order not to arouse suspicion by leaving on the train, he had rented a livery rig one evening, supposedly for a drive in the country. Word had just come in that the team and buggy had been located at Aberdeen and had been left there early the next morning. Mr. Barber was probably in St. Louis or Chicago selling his watches. He had not paid the rent for space in the store, nor for his room and board at the hotel, and even owed whiskey tabs at both saloons. In spite of all this he could not have been all bad. It was reported that he had attended church every Sunday while in Hecla and had been seen to drop a half a dollar in the collection plate each time. Even though his temporary operation did seem to be successful, he never did come back to open the jewelry store.

1906 Stories

I think 1906 was my most "rememberable" year. Some of the events that occurred were so deeply implanted in my memory that they remain as vivid as if they had taken place a few days ago. On the third of July I went with Father to Wolf's for oats to carry the horses through haying. Our crop had been ruined by hail the year before.

It was fun to go along on such trips and, with nothing to do except to ride in the wagon, get him to tell about things when he was a boy. I liked the stories of the trip across the ocean and especially the ones he told of working at the rooming house in Michigan before he had learned to speak English. He would tell of the huge fireplace to which he brought a sled load of wood right into the building each day with a horse. It would be unloaded directly to the fire, and the next morning he would haul the ashes out on the same sled. Then would come the best part. In the evening while he was cleaning things up and the girls were getting the tables ready for breakfast, some of the roomers would coach him in words and messages to say to them. The girls enjoyed the game too and had their own way of keeping most of the bad words out of the interchange. If one of the men got much out of line, he might find a bucket of cold saw dust between his bed blankets or have a cup of hot coffee poured down his back or discover laundry soap in his oatmeal at breakfast. A more severe penalty and the one most fun to watch would take place right after breakfast when the five-minute whistle blew at the saw mill. The men would hurry for their coat and caps that hung on pegs along one side of the room, when the culprit would suddenly find that his had been firmly nailed to the log wall. They were good stories that made the miles and hours pass quickly.

We had dinner with Mr. Wolf, sacked and loaded the grain, and left for home in what seemed to be ample time, but an hour or so later our troubles began. This area, that a few years earlier had been drought stricken, was now plagued by an overabundance of rain. The sub-soil was saturated and some low spots that had carried the empty wagon easily could not support the load. We were stuck in the mud. Father carried the sacks, one by one, on his shoulder to a higher piece of ground ahead until the load was lightened enough for the horses to pull the wagon out. This happened again a mile or so farther on. I was not big enough to even think of carrying a sack of oats, but watching Father and driving the horses while he pushed on the wagon was tiring by itself. We were about three miles from home when we got stuck for the third time. It was getting dark, the horses were as tired as we were, and the mosquitoes swarmed in clouds. It did not take long to decide to unhitch the team, each of us get on a horse and ride home with the plan of coming back early in the morning with four horses instead of two. By daylight we were on our way and although we had no trouble it took longer than we had expected.

The 4th of July Celebration

When we got home Olga and George were waiting for me so the three of us could go to Hecla for the Fourth of July Celebration. Father and Mother were not going since Grandma was not well. I changed clothes as quickly as possible and counted my nickels and dimes when mother gave me an extra half a dollar to spend. Olga and George had already received an equal amount each.

When we got to town we separated, each of us joining up with friends of our own age. The parade had not yet started so we were in time. With a pocket full of money, ice cream, firecrackers, a ball game, a sack race, a three-legged race, and a horse race to watch, the day was over before we knew it. The fireworks came later after we all had gone home for chores and returned. I asked Olga and George if they thought it would be alright for me to stay in town with Bob Mitchell—who already had such permission—and go home with them after the fireworks. They agreed, so Bob and I each bought a can of sardines and some crackers for our supper. Mr. Herther, who owned the store, lent us a can opener and gave us clean wrapping paper to use as plates since it was a common belief that eating from a can was a cause of ptomaine poisoning. We enjoyed our meal on the freight loading platform at the depot and returned the can opener. Mr. Herther invited us in the back room to wash with the remark that we would look a whole lot better and would not draw as many flies. After buying ice cream cones and returning to the depot, we had nothing to do but to loaf and relax until dark and to ponder on the easy life the boys in town must have.

The fireworks were pretty good but were in competition with a thunder storm that was coming in from the west and as a result many of the displays were hurried and overlapping so as to get rid of the stuff before it got wet. We were hardly out of town when the storm caught up with us. There were forks of lightning so bright and continuous that the sky was lighter than day and with thunder claps so sharp and close it seemed as if it was nipping at our wheels. The rain cascaded from the buggy top and the rubber apron buckled in front of us but we kept fairly dry. Father had always told us not to be afraid of lightning because if we could see it, it was past the stage of striking.[12] This was so bright it could be seen through tightly closed eyelids so I leaned first on Olga and then on George and slept all the way home. I had had a busy day.

Barn Fire

In the Spring of the same year, 1906, our dog had been poisoned. Someone gave us a pup as a replacement, and to be sure it was safe we tied it in the barn each night. One night several weeks later Olga awoke and heard it barking. She looked out and saw the barn was on fire. We were all—with the exception of Grandma—out of the house

---

[12] This brings the memory of Ole's brother, George, who was killed by lightning in the field. Ole must have known that the instant death of a lightning strike would not give time for fear.

in no time at all and were met by a sight, the like of which none of us had ever seen and hoped, I am sure, never to see again.

Whoever had started the fire had opened several of the doors and we could see that most of the inside of the barn was alight with new blazes starting as the fire spread. Tongues of flame were licking out of cracks around the eaves and the roof edge, with bigger ones pouring from the louvers of the cupola; as the support of this structure burned away and the pressure from below increased, it suddenly arose twenty or so feet straight up, propelled by a huge column of flame. It hung there a few seconds and then broke up in a shower of sparks and pieces of blazing wood. The shingles floated quite a distance through the air with several of them coming down on the roof of the house.

In seconds George was on the roof beating them out with a wet grain sack. At the same time Mother, Olga, and I formed a bucket brigade from the water tank with Father, halfway up on a ladder, handing the pails to George who slopped the water wherever he could in an effort to keep the roof damp. From time to time, Mother would go in and check on Grandma and come back with the report that she was still asleep. It seemed the house was safe by now unless the wind came up.

By this time the fire was making a steady roar, punctuated by the cracking of the flames and the crashing of sections of the roof and hay-mow, walls, and partitions. Besides the dog the only animals in the barn were two calves and the herd bull, which had a dollar value of more than any ten other animals in the herd. We knew that they were all dead and were glad, at least, that their suffering was over. Then, as we watched the flames and shadows and the grotesque figures they seemed to form, a real shape began to come into view. It was that huge bull, with the appearance of calm deliberation, coming slowly through the wall of fire. On his broad back was a blazing pile of wood and hay from the haymow and being dragged by a chain around his neck was a burning plank that had been part of the manger to which he had been tied. Father shoved the burning mass from his back with something and then poured pailsful of water on him to quench the remaining flames. He then led him a few steps farther on by the ring and found later he had blisters on his fingers from contact with the metal. We hoped for a while that the bull would live but by the next day he was breathing with more difficulty. There was not a hair left on his body and in places the skin and even the flesh was burned so it seemed merciful to put him out of his misery. He stayed on his feet and even followed the pressure on his ring to a distance far enough from the house for burial.

The fire started at two o'clock. By daylight there was nothing left but ashes and a few small flames here and there. Our first job was to build temporary fences so the livestock from the pasture could have access to the water tank and to arrange some kind of an enclosure in which to hold the milk cows for the morning milking. Chores had to be done.

It became a long day. From mid-morning on, neighbors were coming and going to see the ruins, to offer the loan of things we might need, and to help if they could. Some pitched in to help reinforce the fence we had hurriedly put up at daybreak, others helped to dig a grave for the big bull, while some set poles for the frame of a temporary shelter in which to feed and harness the work horses.

One of the last persons to come was Jim Keefe, a dissolute sort of an individual, who worked for Charlie Johnson. He was very drunk and having a great deal of trouble with his speech and his equilibrium but did manage to kneel and maintain that position while he stated his willingness to swear on a stack of Bibles that he did not set the fire. He added that he had been home and in bed at midnight, two hours before the fire started. Charlie Johnson said afterwards that he came in after four o'clock and was so drunk he could not get him up at chore time. Anyway, Jim packed his belongings and left that night. It was reported a few months later that he had lost his life in a construction accident at Mobridge.

The loss of the bull, the barn, and all the contents was staggering. It became worse by the fact that insurance had been carried on the buildings for years, but the policy had expired a few days before and had not yet been renewed. Besides our loss, a brand-new buggy and a set of driving harnesses, belonging to a vacationing Methodist minister, had been destroyed.

One of Father's favorite sayings, of which he had many, was, "It's no use to cry over spilt milk." He applied this by borrowing a team the next day, going to town and coming home with halters, three sets of work harnesses, and lumber to make mangers and feed boxes in the horse shed. Fortunately, our saddles, according to summer custom, were kept in the well house and were not lost. On the third day we went back to the hayfield. After all, we had hay to put up and two days of good weather had been spent at other things.

Another quotation Father used was, "There is no loss so great but what there is some gain." The only gain I could find was my personal pleasure in the new harnesses. My team, Captain and Jake, were the equal of any circus team and we bucked hay[13] accordingly. I would have welcomed a new saddle too but knew this was no time to try to promote one.

The new barn was built and in use by winter.

Death of Grandma

During the winter and through spring it could be seen that Grandma was failing. She spent more time in her rocking chair, with even an occasional nap on her bed, and did not object when others took over some of the work she had always claimed as her own.

---

[13] This involves a lot of cooperative labor from both man and horses: cutting the hay, laying it in rows to dry, stacking bundles into a hay stack, and then transporting the hay to the hay barn to use as feed.

Although she tried to seem interested in what each of us had done, she often had trouble keeping awake while we answered her questions. The gardening and hatching of baby chickens had been her responsibility other years, but when planting time came she said she was not up to it. Her eyesight worsened so that she could no longer read her Bible, so Father, Mother, or sometimes Olga would read to her, but usually she would be asleep after a couple of verses. She said she knew something unusual was happening the night of the fire but it is doubtful if she ever realized the barn was gone.

About that time we began taking a saddle horse with us to the hayfield and during the noon hour Father or Olga would ride home to see how things were. Then one night, about three weeks later, I heard voices and Olga going down the stairs. I was not called at the customary time, but an hour or so later Olga came upstairs to tell me that Grandma was very weak and we would not go to the hayfield that day. Grandma died at about eleven o'clock.

We did not yet have a telephone so I was sent north to tell some of the neighbors while George rode to Houghton for the same purpose and to call Reverend Glesne, at Aberdeen, on the telephone. When I got back, a couple of neighbor women were already there and Father was leaving for Hecla, driving a team and the single seated buggy. He came home later in the afternoon with the undertaker's lightweight utility wagon which was used as a hearse for country funerals. It was loaded with a rough-box and a coffin. Neighbors helped unload the latter and place it on sawhorses back of the drapes which covered the double doorway into the sitting room.

The next morning Father drove to the cemetery at Houghton where friends helped place the rough-box in the grave they had dug. George and I tried to figure out some useful jobs to do, but there was a lot of activity around the house with neighbor women helping, and every time we came in sight there would be some extra chore for us. So we saddled up, fixed a lunch, and rode over to check the east pastures. It seemed like about the simplest and most worthwhile thing we could do.

The following day was the funeral. George and I oiled the double buggy, and when he had harnessed the horses, I cleaned the sweat stains from the harnesses and polished the metalwork. Since my team was to pull the buggy, I knew I would be the driver and wanted everything to look as shiny as possible.

The service at the house was over by about one-thirty and we were ready to start on the long, slow trip to the cemetery. In front, ahead of the dust and setting the pace, was Reverend Glesne. Next came the hearse driven by Jim Johnson and then the family with Father and me in the front seat and Mother, Olga, and George in the rear. Behind us were six or seven neighbor rigs with a couple joining us along the way. At first, after the days of rest, the horses had to be held back as they were curious about the unusual vehicle ahead of them but soon settled down to conform with the dust and heat of the August afternoon.

Quite a gathering of friends from the Houghton neighborhood were at the cemetery when we arrived. The horses were tied to the fence and the minister conducted a second service. The coffin was lowered and the lid placed on the rough-box. One of the men stepped down on a short ladder to insert the screws to hold it in place. As he came up another gave him a hand and in so doing loosened several clods of earth which echoed as they fell on the lid with an awesome sound as if thunder was coming up out of the grave. Father turned and walked away a few steps and I could see he was crying. I wished I could have comforted him, but of course, I did not know the words or how to say them, when suddenly I realized that had I known, it would have been impossible for me to do so because I was busy on my own trying to choke back uncontrollable sobs that kept coming up in my throat.

To hide my emotion, I hurried to the horses on the pretense of seeing they were still securely tied. Father came over about then and said he was glad I was getting ready to leave. He helped to untie the team and cautioned me to keep a good hold on Jake in case someone should suddenly open a parasol and startle him into showing off. As Father went over to shake hands with friends and neighbors, I turned the buggy around and was kind of pleased when Jake did act up a little and I could control him with a tight rein and a voice which I hoped sounded gruff and several octaves lower than it really was. The trip home did not take long. George rode with Jim, and when we got to the house, he quickly changed clothes and continued on to Hecla to return the hearse to the undertaker and bring back the buggy.

That night the events of the preceding days whirled through my mind so fast I was afraid I never would go to sleep and it kind of worried me. I am sure Olga realized this because she came to my room, across the hall from hers, and explained that she was not sleepy either and would probably be awake for hours. Before she did go to sleep, she said she would come in and see how I was getting along. With this assurance I closed my eyes and knew nothing more until daylight and the call that started every working day, "Fred, it is time to bring in the horses." After all, we had hay to put up and were behind three more days.

Carl—Hired Man

One of the most memorable of Father's and Mother's traits was their readiness to befriend anyone in need. So, when Reverend Glesne called on the telephone in mid-January of 1907 and told of a Norwegian sailor who was to be released from the hospital in Aberdeen, who had no money and no place to go for a period of convalescence, their response was not surprising. They said to put him on the train for Hecla and they would meet him when he arrived.

I remember him only as "Carl." His last name and the story of how he got to Dakota in the middle of the winter are forgotten. He

42

was a likeable young man with interesting things to tell of the places he had been and the things he had seen. He taught George and me how to make a splice in a rope so smooth it could hardly be detected and many knots and hitches and their practical uses. As his strength returned, he tried more and more to help with the work and managed quite often to demonstrate how certain chores should not be done.

The principal and all-important winter work was to haul in hay for the daily feeding of two to three hundred head of cattle. The first chore each morning after breakfast was to take a load of hay through the barnyard to the pasture and, with the team maintaining a slow walk, unload it over a large enough area that all the animals could have access to it. Then back through the barnyard and to the hayfield for a load for the next morning. "Loading," or building a square load on a hayrack in a way that it balances on the sled, takes a lot of practice, but Carl had been along often enough that he said he could manage. So one cold morning he was allowed to take the hay to the pasture. Going through the one gate he caught the post with his load and broke it off. As father was pulling the gate out of the way he looked and saw that he had unloaded the hay in one huge pile. This necessitated a quick re-loading job before it was all trampled underfoot and wasted. Going back through the barnyard he caught one more gate post and the corner of the barn. In spite of the indication of an unlucky day, he persuaded Father to allow him to go alone for the day's load just to show that he could do something right. In a couple of hours he came back, standing on the front bob of the sled with the fork held high over his head and the horse on a dead gallop. He said his load had capsized.

With closer supervision he did quite well for a while, or until the episode of the windmill. Between the house and the barn was a windmill on top of a thirty-foot wooden tower. The well was no longer in use but the machinery was in good shape. It had been sold and the buyer was expected any day to dismantle it and lower it to the ground piece by piece. The lumber in the tower would be salvaged and used for repairs of all sorts. Father mentioned to Carl that when the mill was taken down he could have the job of taking the tower apart. Then one afternoon while Father and Mother were in town, he took it upon himself to complete the whole thing in one maneuver. Stored in the barn was a lot of rope used to run the hay stacker in the summer. With one end of this tied to the top of the tower and the other fastened to posts inside of the barn, Carl hoped to lower the structure to the ground so that it could be worked on easily. As with so many well laid plans, it failed. The whole thing came down with a crash, the windmill barely missing the house, and the broken posts on the other end of the rope luckily missing him. With his usual remark of not crying over spilt milk, Father hauled the ruined machinery out of the way and on his next trip to town bought a buck-saw and assigned Carl to sawing the tower up for stove wood.

In late March Carl became anxious to return to the sea. Father took him to town, bought him a ticket to Chicago where he was sure he could find work, and gave him enough money to carry him over until he could find a suitable job. He probably had a feeling of satisfaction in having carried through a good deed but, no doubt, a greater sense of relief in seeing the train pulling out and realizing that Carl was on board.

Some weeks later we had a letter from Carl. He had signed up in Chicago for a seaman's job in New York with train fare advanced, was now on a good ship, and appreciated the care he had had during the winter. He really was a nice person.

Ole takes George to Chicago

This year, 1907, was the year Father took a vacation. This was unusual because in the memory of all of us except Mother he had never even thought of such a thing before. She, of course, remembered his trip to Denmark with the stops, both going and coming, in Chicago before they were married. He had gone many times to Chicago or Sioux City for days at a time with shipments of livestock, but these were not carefree outings. Instead, these were days of deep concern during which he hoped none of his animals would be injured in shipping, wondering if he had happened on a good market, deciding whether to accept the first bid or to instruct the commission firm to hold the animals another day, and the many other cares incident to shipping and marketing of livestock.

So, about the first of June Father and George went to Chicago where they spent a week or so with relatives. George came home with stories of tall buildings, trolley cars, and automobiles, but impressed mostly by the speed and accuracy of the players in executing double plays in the two major league baseball games he had seen. From there they went to Michigan to visit Father's oldest brother and family. He had been the first to come to America and had settled there to a life of farming. Here George was amazed at how a family could get along on a farm of eighty acres compared to ours, which would make twenty-five of that size.

Unbeknownst to Father and George, Mother had arranged with her nephew, John Thomsen of Clinton, Iowa,[14] —a young man in his early twenties who had adopted the trade of house painting—to come up and paint the new barn while they were away. He was a good worker and with some help, the value of which is questionable, from Olga and me the job was quickly done. In comparison the house now looked shabby, so Mother and John went to town and bought paint for it as a double surprise for the travelers who returned in about three weeks, all vacationed out and glad to be home.

Out of Debt

This was a good year and in looking back I am sure it was of greater moment than I realized at the time. I believe it was the year Father and Mother reached their goal and were finally out of debt.

---

[14] This was John N. Thomsen, son of Sophia and John's brother, Niels.

Money was still spent carefully, but many things were bought that year that previously would have been studied upon longer, such as new furniture for the house, a new surrey and driving harness for transportation, and for me a saddle I had long admired.

In the Spring of 1908 Olga graduated from High School and in the Fall entered the School of Medicine at the University of Minnesota. These two events made a good reason for a vacation, both as a graduation present and to learn a little about the University and its surroundings before the classes began. Mother and Olga left in June for Chicago, where they visited friends and Mother's sister and her son whom she had not seen for years. From there they went to Clinton, Iowa, to spend a few days with Mother's brother and family, of which John, the painter of the preceding year, was a member. They were in Minneapolis several days during which Olga learned many details of her chosen course of study, became somewhat familiar with the campus, and found a satisfactory place to room and board. They were home in time for the start of haying. This was Olga's last season in the hayfield and, in fact, the last summer that any of us would put up a crop of hay in South Dakota. If anyone had made such a prediction at that time, none of us would have believed it.

Departure for Bird Island, Minnesota

1909 began like any other year except that there was a land boom on. There had been several years of heavy rainfall and as a result crops were exceptionally good. There were instances where individuals had bought a quarter of a section of land and had grown enough flax to pay for it in one year. Farmers, like Father, who had shied away from grain were being tempted. In fact, he did have a crop of flax followed by one of wheat. Both turned out well, but he and Mother remembered the drought of twenty years before and did not really feel secure. With buyers from Iowa and other states increasing in numbers, the prices of land went to what seemed an unbelievable level. Several offers had been refused for the land upon which the buildings were located. When this offer was made to include the entire holdings, Father and Mother did not hesitate to sell. They could have retired comfortably on what they received but instead chose to find another farm and keep busy a few more years.

In looking for a place, they answered many advertisements in farm papers and visited several states, finally deciding on eight hundred acres at Bird Island, Minnesota, about ninety miles west of Minneapolis. This would be convenient for Olga to come home for vacations and for George, who planned on attending the Agricultural College at St. Paul after his two or more years of high school.

Instead of putting up hay that summer, the time was spent with the many things that had to be done before we could move. When it became known that our Galloway herd was to be sold, there was an unusual demand for breeding stock. We then selected the thirty-five or so registered animals we intended to take with us. The remainder of the herd was sorted into different classes and shipped to the market in Chicago. Next we went over the horses, selling many of the lighter ones or trading some of them for heavier animals that had been brought in by recent arrivals to the neighborhood. It was believed these would fit in well with the farming in Minnesota. When it came time to ship, we had about thirty-five head, from a Percheron[15] stallion down to colts that had just been weaned. Some of the farm machinery had been sold, the grain harvested and threshed, and it was time to take the first actual step in moving.

The farming operation in Minnesota would be much different from what we were used to. It would be mostly raising small grain such as wheat, oats, and barley. In order to get the seeding done as early as possible in the Spring, the fields had to be plowed the preceding Fall. With a minimum of three hundred acres to prepare, and one man with five horses doing well to average four acres a day,

---

[15] A breed of draft horse that originated in western France.

this job loomed bigger and bigger. For some reason which I do not remember, possession of the property in South Dakota would definitely not be given until a certain date in the latter part of October. So it was decided that about the first of September George would ship with the two rail cars of horses and equipment to Bird Island, buy plows, extra harnesses and horse feed, hire a man, and get the fall plowing under way. Even yet it seems like a pretty big assignment for a seventeen-year-old, but he was resourceful, had always welcomed responsibility, and so made out quite well.

In order to save the transferring the cars from one railroad line to another at Aberdeen, it was thought best to load at Groton, east of Aberdeen and thirty some miles almost due south of our place. On the designated morning we left home after an early breakfast, with Father driving the wagon, which was loaded with harnesses, horse equipment, and several sacks of oats for horse feed. Two horses were tied directly behind the wagon and back of each of these were five more, each one tied firmly to the tail of the animal ahead. Then there were twenty some colts and other loose animals, followed by George and me trying to keep the bunch intact and moving and out of mischief. Father and George had been over the route a few days before when they had gone to Groton to order the cars and had found places where they could Zig or Zag over open fields and avoid, as much as possible, farm buildings and horse pastures.

At one farm place which we could not bypass, we did have considerable trouble when a washing on a line scattered the loose horses so that it took an hour or more and several miles of hard riding to gather them in again. With this in mind, we approached the depot in Groton with some fear that they might scatter among all the houses and buildings in town. This problem did not materialize, however, because a great number of people had lined up along the road to help guide the animals into the loading pens nearby. Whether to give us a helping hand or, as some of them said, to protect their own yards and gardens, the help was appreciated. By pre-

48

arrangement the mangers had been filled with hay, so we watered and grained the horses and went to the restaurant for a well-deserved meal. It was now the middle of the afternoon and although we had munched a couple of sandwiches, we were hungry.

Father was going to stay overnight to help George with the loading, so after dinner I saddled a long-legged bay mare who had an unweaned colt waiting at home and started on my return trip. I had intended to follow the main roads but with everything strange to me I ran into difficulties and when I got back on our old trail again, I let the mare choose the way. I had all I could do to hold her back to a reasonable gait, and every so often she would raise her head and let out a shrill whinny for that pesky colt. They must have heard each other for many miles because Mother said she heard us coming in the dark for at least four miles. Mother had done all the necessary chores and I was glad to have no more to do than to unsaddle and feed the mare, eat supper, and go to bed. I had probably ridden eighty-five or more miles that day and was about as tired as I ever had been in all my fourteen years—unless maybe when I was real small and had been to the circus.

Father came home shortly after noon the next day having seen George on his way in good shape. With the horse he rode, we had a team with which to do whatever work was necessary. Until a week or so before we left there was not a great deal for us to do, so I decided to dig and sell the potatoes we had planted for winter and which would now go to waste. I managed to sell some good-sized lots to the stores, hotel, and restaurant and then began peddling from house to house until I just about gutted the market in Hecla. It was hard work but paid off quite well. I did not keep the money long, however, but spent most of it for a new saddle, which I really did not need.

The last few days before our departure were filled with real hard work. This time the cars were to be shipped from Hecla. With the help of neighbors, the cattle were driven to the loading pens, and we hauled the other belongings that were to be taken and loaded them in a box car. They were stacked and anchored down in both ends of the car, with the middle section well bedded with hay and reserved for the team and the colt. Father and I would sleep there too. Mother was to spend a few days with friends before following us.

I was pleased when the train crew invited me to ride in the top of the caboose for a last view of Hecla on the morning we left. Ten minutes later I had some misgivings about the whole thing as the train crossed the west end of the pasture, which was now empty, and where so many times before, this same train had blown its whistle and either scattered the horses I was trying to gather or hurried them towards home, depending upon the mood they were in that day. I knew that our farm buildings a mile east were empty, too. It was not long before we were past Aberdeen and speeding east on the main line, with the thrill of adventure dispelling any apprehensions I might have had. At dark we bedded down in the hay with the colt trying to contest my choice of the softest spot. When I awoke we were in Bird Island, our home for the next four years.

South Dakota Memories

Before ending this, I must list a few South Dakota memories which I shall never forget. They include the mirages that occurred quite often on still summer mornings and brought towns and buildings from far away to appear to be within a stone's throw; the Northern Lights so brilliant that we, as children, knew they must originate just north of Hecla; a winter morning after a heavy snowfall, with the pasture a pure unmarred white, when one by one the cattle would stand, shake off their blankets of snow, and merge into a black herd on its way to meet the hay sled; a number of horses walking in a protective circle around a cow with a newborn calf and a pair of coyotes lurking in the background; a stormy winter evening with the family in the sitting room under the huge hanging lamp and in the friendly glow of the hard coal heater with the isinglass doors and, whether we realized or not, being very fortunate; and a general ring on the party line telephone with Carl Knutson playing his latest "Edison Record" over the wire. It seemed, in the field of communication and technology, we had gone about as far as we could go.

If sometime someone will find something of interest in this rambling recital, my purpose will have been accomplished. If not, and it finds its way to the incinerator, it has not been a total loss. The fun I have had in reviving and reliving these, and other associated incidents, has been well worth the effort.

*　*　*　*

Among the tombstones bearing the names of friends and neighbors, in the neatly kept cemetery at Houghton, is one of sturdy, polished granite with the inscription HANSEN and nothing else. In the surrounding plot are the graves of Grandma, Father, Mother, and George, and my two uncles, Fred and George. It is a peaceful spot.

Completed at

Independence, Missouri

June 30, 1975

Frederic W. Hansen

Born at Hecla, South Dakota

June 30, 1895

Chapter 2

Bird Island, Minnesota, by Fred Hansen

Fred continues his narrative with his high school years 1909 to 1913 in Bird Island, Minnesota, about ninety miles due west of Minneapolis.

Not long ago, I wrote things I remembered from my earliest years in South Dakota, where I was born. I shall now try to describe happenings from my memory of the four years during which we lived at Bird Island, Minnesota, following our departure from South Dakota. There were great changes taking place everywhere at that time but, of course, we did not realize it then. It was the beginning of the end of the so-called, "Horse and Buggy Days."

Life in Bird Island, Minnesota

The move from the grass covered prairie at Hecla to the strictly farming community at Bird Island in the Fall of 1909, when I was fourteen, brought changes to our family way of life also. Although the work was as hard and the days as long, the tasks did not seem to be as demanding. Perhaps the fact that I was growing and not so far behind George in size and strength, together with the novelty of new surroundings and entirely different methods of farming, had much to do with my feelings.

We all enjoyed the proximity of town and the ability to go in for errands in minutes as compared with the visits to Hecla, which would spoil a half a day at any time of the year. I believe this meant more to Mother than to the rest of us in that she was soon associated with Ladies' Aids and Betterment groups, and could attend meetings whenever she chose without problems or worries. George and I relished the ease with which we could get to school and the chance to take in evening entertainments, athletic events, and social activities. Olga was at the University in Minneapolis but came home for holidays and Summer vacations. She fitted into the family life at Bird Island during those periods, although her "roots" were probably beginning to set in Minneapolis.

The Farm and Farm Work

A great change took place in Father. In the past, as was his inherent right and duty, he had always taken on the most unpleasant jobs, had put in the longest days in the heat of Summer and most hours in the Winter's cold. Now he suddenly assumed the combined roles of general manager, handy man, and chore boy. He was always busy, as he called it, puttering around. He did not hesitate to tackle anything, no matter how tough it seemed, but I do not remember him ever putting in a day in the field. With his driving team he was always ready for a trip to town to purchase supplies or repairs or to hire an extra man or to bring needed materials to the field so as to avoid delays in the work. He enjoyed it but, no doubt, was deeply thankful his financial assets were such that he could buy implements and equipment for the farm without worrying about how he could pay for it, as he had done so many times in the past.

George, having organized the work on the farm before the rest of us arrived, continued to take a great part in the decisions of management, the rotation of crops, and the assignments of work. Having acceded to his more mature judgment for as long as I could remember, I readily accepted this arrangement. He and I worked and got along well together with, of course, an occasional minor difference of opinion. These usually had to do with the sale or use of certain horses or teams to which I was particularly attached but were always settled quickly and amicably.

The farm of eight hundred acres was actually composed of two adjoining farms. The home place, upon which we lived, contained four hundred and eighty acres. It continued for a mile along the east village limits of Bird island and also east from town for a mile with the ends of this right angle being a half a mile across. The other farm of three hundred and twenty acres was a half a mile wide and continued on for another mile east. Thus the area was in the shape of an L, two miles long and with a base of one mile.

The owners of the home farm had, some years before, built it up into somewhat of a showplace with an unusually large barn, an old but good house and plenty of outbuildings for any need. These were located at the junction of the upright of the L and the base and not far from the village limits.

The buildings of the other farm, known as the Poore farm because of the name of the previous owner, were a mile straight east of Bird Island. A middle aged, semi-retired brother of the owner lived there with his wife. When Father bought the place, he invited them to stay in the knowledge that occupied farm buildings would not deteriorate as those that were vacant. In the busy haying and harvest seasons, we stabled our work horses there and made the trip from home in a lighter rig, thus saving the work teams some miles or hours of "horse energy." At these times Mr. Poore would help to take care of the horses and feed them early enough in the mornings so all we had to do upon arrival was to harness up and go to work. Although there was no spoken agreement, we repaid him by keeping the barn filled with hay and feed for his two cows and one driving horse so as to carry them through the winters. It was a good arrangement, and one that lasted for the four years we lived at Bird Island. During that time both parties claimed to have had the best end of the bargain.

With automobiles slowly increasing in numbers, many of the old horse men conceded that the machines had some merit and, although they could never replace driving horses, they might in time become a useful means of Summer transportation if enough gravel could be found to surface the dirt roads and make rainy weather travel possible. This would do a lot for the buggies and wagons too. Some, who had ridden in automobiles, said the thrill of speeding along at thirty or more miles an hour was an experience not to be forgotten. But even with this interest in motors beginning to grow, the heavy farm equipment such as the tractor, the truck, and the harvesting combine were not yet in use.

Horse Power

The power that produced the crops on the farm was strictly horse and mule power. Horses hauled the logs from the woods for the nation's lumber, built the grades for the railroads and highways, moved the Army and, except for huge steam engines and water falls, were the source of energy upon which civilization depended. There were thousands of horses in the large cities performing every task imaginable from delivering groceries to pulling fire engines. The latter were the most spectacular with the training to move from their stalls to their places under the suspended harnesses and to be on a gallop down the street within thirty seconds from the sound of the alarm.

The greatest number of horses in the cities were used by the transfer and moving companies to handle the loads of freight that are moved by trucks today. They were driven in teams of from two to six animals pulling vans of all sizes and description. It was a memorable sight to see a teamster back his six-horse van to a loading dock amid the din and clatter of busy traffic, with the ears of his horses attuned only to his voice and their responses keyed to his firm but easy pressure on the reins, with the same degree of accuracy and precision as that of a modern truck driver using power steering, power brakes, and side view mirrors.

The yelling jerking, slap-dash pictures seen on TV of horses being driven is a slight upon the memory of the teamsters whose art has gone with the advance of progress. Gone too are the animal odors, the millions of flies, the clouds of sparrows and the sanitation department employees, who with their barrel-like carts, brooms, and shovels did their best to keep the streets of the cities passably clean. But this soliloquy has already gone too far. I shall now return to my attempt to tell of some of the incidents that occurred at Bird Island during the family's four years there.

School in Bird Island

By the time we were settled so George and I could start school, the term had been under way for six of seven weeks. I was not anxious to begin my first year of high school that far behind in a class made up of strangers and in a new school and offered many good, sound reasons why it would be better to stay out a year and start with a new class later. Mother voted each one down promptly in her firm belief that to needlessly miss a day of school was an unforgivable sin. George was not greatly concerned and, with two years of high school behind him, was sure it would turn out alright. It did. With the help of teachers and classmates, we soon caught up with the work and began to feel like full-fledged members of the institution.

At first we took a shortcut through the pasture to save a few blocks. Then George decided to jog the distance each day. He said it cleared his mind. I felt that anyone who would run to school when he could just as well ride a horse had a mind that needed something and so began looking for a barn near the school. I found one that was owned by a man who still had a cow but empty horse stalls. We made a deal by which I would bring in a team and haul away the pile of manure that had accumulated in the alley and repeat the cleanup job in the Spring. This agreement lasted for my four years of high school. If the weather was bad George occasionally rode, and once in a while we took a team and a light sled, but, as a rule, he jogged the shortcut and I rode the long way with both of us arriving at about the same time. We often walked to town in the evenings at a reasonable rate of speed. Presumably his mind did not need clearing at that time of day.

Winter Fun

With Olga coming home for Thanksgiving and the Christmas and Easter vacations, school parties, basketball games, and all such things the winter passed quickly. George and I contributed some to the fun by occasionally loading the big bobsled with hay and blankets and taking a group of friends for a sleigh ride. At these times I always, by choice, drove the horses. I liked the sound of the sleigh bells, the slap of the horseshoes on the hard packed snow of Main Street, and the crunch of the runners on the sharp curves as much as some of the giggling that came up from the sled box. It was not that I disliked girls. I had no trouble finding partners to ride on the seat under the heavy lap robe. Some even liked to drive, and all said they had had a good time. I believed this although I sometime wondered if they envied their giggling friends in the blankets and the hay. Anyway, it was fun and a good winter.

Flax

With the end of the school term, there was also a lull in the activities on the farm. The main crops had all been planted and were growing but the corn was not yet big enough to cultivate. The brood mares had been given a vacation to run with their colts in the pasture as were the three-year-olds after their first season in harness. Farmers repaired fences and buildings and did other odd jobs and some even took off a day now and then and went fishing. George and I carried out a plan we had talked about all winter.

About a hundred acres of the home farm had, at one time, been a lake. This had deteriorated long ago until it was no more than a big slough, which had been drained several years ago by a county ditch. The soil was spongy and the grass too course to be of much value but the area was included in the pasture. We fenced off ten acres or so, plowed it, and sowed flax. This crop grew best on newly broken sod, but care had to be taken so it would not be put in before the danger of frost was past. With this done it was time to continue with the routine fieldwork.

Reverend Glesne and his Model T Ford

One afternoon, a couple of weeks later, we were caught in a heavy shower, came in from the field, stabled the horses, and wondered what kind of a suitable job we could find to complete the day. Then a Model T Ford came slithering down the road and stopped in the yard. We recognized all the Glesne family from Aberdeen, South Dakota.

Reverend Glesne was a stern and exacting Norwegian Lutheran minister who was the Pastor of the Church at Houghton. In 1904 Olga had been a member of one of his confirmation classes and George in one four years later. Among our books is a Bible with the inscription in Mother's handwriting, "George N. Hansen, June 14, 1908. Confirmation present." I do not remember much about George's catechismal training except the joke that, presumably started with Martin Luther, to the effect the pre-confirmation year of a teenage boy was the hardest of his life because he was considered too big to cry and not yet old enough to swear. This did not apply to girls because, as everyone knew, girls did not swear, and even if they felt the urge, they did not know the dirty words that had become a part of profanity. Now, in 1909, it was time for me to start the training. I attended one session and then by devious means and stretching the truth out of all proportion managed to find excuses for missing the next three. I knew there would be a day of reckoning when, suddenly, we were getting ready to move to Minnesota and nothing more was said about my "reading for the minister."

For a moment, as Reverend Glesne stepped from the car, I thought again about the day of reckoning but soon realized he had too many problems of his own to worry about or even notice an unconfirmed adolescent who also had a sneaky streak. The Glesnes had been on the way for three miserable days with the intention of visiting relatives in Wisconsin. The only roads were of dirt with occasionally a span of gravel on the main street of some town. These roads often petered down to nothing but two wheel ruts in the prairie. There were, of course, no filling stations with rest rooms nor road maps. They had a railroad timetable with an outline of the railroad giving the names of the stations and often asked the way from town to town. On top of that it had rained every day. They were tired, wet, and discouraged.

Father and Mother invited them to stay and rest as long as they wished when Father came up with the best idea yet. He suggested they leave the car, continue the trip by train and maybe by the time they returned the rainy spell would be over. This was agreed upon. George and I had been looking for something to do and so with brooms, buckets and rags washed the mud from the car. We then opened the door to an empty driveway in the barn and Reverend Glesne drove it in. Just as were leaving he stepped back and removed the ignition key, explaining to Father that without it no one could start the motor. He then said something about a temptation to these two boys.

A couple of days later a similar car came into the yard and George removed the key and made a pattern on a piece of cardboard. It did not take long to make a key although we learned afterwards that a piece of wire bent in the shape of a U could have been used. The next Sunday Father, Mother, and Olga went to church. It did not take long for us to start the Model T. We took turns driving and soon handled it quite well. After about four miles up and down the road we were within a hundred feet of the barn when the motor coughed and died. We were out of gas.

I hurried to the well house where we kept a barrel of gasoline, drew off a couple of gallons and came back by the time George had found the gas tank under the front seat. We were busy pouring in the fuel when the surrey, with the folks home from church, pulled up beside us. Father was always easy to get along with and had overlooked many harmless pranks. But this was no harmless prank and he did not hesitate to tell us so and that he was very much disappointed in us and ashamed of what we had done. His words cut deeply and hurt and made us feel uncomfortable for a long time because they were true.

When the family returned, Reverend Glesne checked the car and prepared to start it. He brought the ignition key from his purse and again spoke of the importance of this small piece of metal that had the power to start and stop this powerful engine. Father nodded in agreement and then remarked that if he would show the boys the location of the gasoline tank, they would fill it for his return trip. He could not help chuckling over his own joke and to hide it turned to us with a smile. We knew we had been forgiven.

Harvest

The latter part of July, we began preparing for the harvest, the busiest time of the year on the farm. The horses had been worked just enough to be in the best condition and we were anxious to start this new experience. Mother had stocked up on groceries and kitchen equipment and arranged for help with her work. Father had bought two new grain binders, each drawn by five horses and cutting a swath of eight feet. As George and I followed each other around each field, we figured that after twenty miles each day we had cut approximately forty acres. We could easily keep ahead of three men following us and setting the bundles up in shocks.

Our main problem for the first couple of weeks was keeping enough men. There was no shortage of help. The freight trains going west were loaded with harvest hands. The trains all stopped at the coal chute, about two blocks from the corner of our farm, for fuel, so it was an ideal spot for these men to unload, work a day or two, and catch another train towards the west where farms were larger and the season longer. A few even came out in the evening, asked for work, and left after breakfast.

There were stories of agitators and troublemakers, but we had only one of them and he was not very good at it. He came over just about quitting time one evening and asked George if he thought he could get a job if he went to the house and asked and then wanted to know what kind of place it was to work. He replied the food was good, the pay was prompt, but that loafing would not be tolerated. By the time we unhitched and got to the buildings, he was hired and waiting for supper. In the morning he went to the field with the other two men who were real good workers.

As we came around the field we saw that he had done very little work and that it was done poorly. Across the field we saw he was standing and talking most of time so on the next round George stopped and asked what the trouble was. He quickly answered that he was urging the others to slow down and suggested that George do the same and make the job last longer and the work easier. With this George stepped down from the seat on the binder reached in the tool box for a handy monkey wrench and told him he was fired.

It surprised him so to find he had been talking to a member of the family that he stood and listened to the choices that were offered. First, if he thought he had wages coming he could go to the house, explain why he was fired and then ask for his money. If he felt he did not deserve any money and that it was his lucky day, he could turn around and head for the railroad track right now. He quickly decided on the second option and left with the only sign of speed he had shown all morning.

We soon began getting better help, and by the time we were stacking the grain we had a crew of six dependable men besides George and me. Some of them came back in following years. One man brought his grown son the next time and, by prearrangement, a daughter the next year, to help in the kitchen.

With the grain stacked, usually in "settings" of four or six stacks, threshing could be taken care of any time later when it was convenient. George and I would soon go back to school but we would stay out a few days to help at threshing time. Two full-time hired men began plowing to prepare for next year's crop. Except for corn picking, in November and December, about the only harvesting yet to do was our small ten-acre field of flax.

Showing at the County Fair

Our Galloway cattle, with their black, curly hair and uniform stocky build, attracted considerable attention. Early in the spring someone from the Fair Board asked Father if he would care to show some of them at the Grenville County Fair, which would be held at Bird Island in September; if so, the breed would be included in the entry list. He turned the decision over to George and me. He talked to the officials and explained that these animals had never been haltered, tied, or led and so it would be impossible to show them in the usual way. We suggested a fair-sized pen, attached to one of the cattle barns, in which they could run loose, and promised to keep it clean and well bedded and to do all we could to maintain an acceptable and interesting exhibit.

This was agreed upon, and so a couple of days before Fair time we drove about fifteen head to the grounds, a distance of not over a half mile. We told the history, traits, and merits of the breed to anyone who was interested but made no converts and sold no breeding stock. Everything went well and it was fun. The cattle judge, a specialist from the State University, was pleased with the arrangement and realized the animals represent choice types of the breed. As a result, we accumulated a large number of blue ribbons and would receive a substantial amount of prize money. Our enterprise had been a success.

Horse Racing at the County Fair

One of the highlights of the fair was the horse racing. There was an excellent half-mile track, a large grandstand and large enough purses to attract well-known names of both horses and drivers. It was all harness racing, except, at the very last, a running race[16] was scheduled to please some of the local people. For some unknown reason, this was run in three heats, as the preceding races had been, amounting to three separate races with prizes paid for each one. The real winnings—and losses—were from bets made by owners, riders, and their supporters. George and I talked this over and decided to pay the entry fee and take part. At home we had a beautiful, dark bay mare that was the fastest thing we had ever ridden. Father had gotten her in a trade with some traveling Gypsies a couple of years before and for some reason had given her to me. Having been "trading stock," she had her share of faults and shortcomings, some physical and some temperamental. The name "Gyp," which I gave her, seemed to fit real well. Her most important defect was a stiffness in her front legs following a spell of overexertion. Next in importance was a nervousness that often came on if she was overheated or excited. During one of these attacks, she might become nearly unmanageable. Otherwise, if used with judgment, she was a gentle and well-behaved driving mare. But, as we knew, she could run.

While George signed up for the race, I rode the pony home and led Gyp back just about in time for the first heat. He had been unable to get any bets since the strangers were somewhat leery of an unknown horse. The first heat was easy. George held her in just enough to win and so, at least, recovered the entry fee. During the intermission, or period until the next heat, I stayed around the barn where I had stabled Gyp and my saddle horse while George again tried to raise a few side bets, with no results.

When we started for the track, we noticed she had already begun to stiffen in her front legs but hoped she would come out of it by the time we reached the entrance gate. She was slow in starting, however, and did not reach her full stride until about halfway around the track. By then George realized he probably could not win

---

[16] A rider on the horse.

anyway so he held her in, satisfied to come in with the losers.

When he reached the barn he told me to get on my horse and to lead Gyp slowly around the grounds until the next round and not let her stop for a single instant. As I went forth and back from the far end of the grounds to the stable, I noticed there were two places she especially wanted to go: the home stable or the fairgrounds. I saw too that her eyes were getting kind of wild and she was sweating up a lather. But her legs stayed loose and I was not worried about George not being able to ride her.

When the call came and he mounted, he showed me a card with names and dollar figures of bets he had made. At a quick glance it looked like well over a hundred dollars, an amount near to what we would receive in cattle prizes. Everything was looking up. At the gate, Gyp refused to enter the track but I was still on my horse and led her through. A moment later the starter yelled, "Go," and the race was on.

At the quarter pole, Gyp was leading by a good two lengths and at the half by two more. At the three-quarter mark she was running as she had never run before, and coming into the home stretch there was no way she could lose except by flying off the track. But she had seen the gate that led to the barn and began pulling to the right. George reached under her neck so as to get both reins in his left hand for better leverage but could not budge her. He then held his hat over her right eye and finally began fanning her with it on the right side of her head but she had figured her trajectory well and hit the gate about in the center, scattering boards and spectators alike.

She stumbled but was on her feet in a second and heading for the barn with George hanging to the bit with both hands but not slackening her at all. I arrived at the same time, ready for instructions. I was to take her home as quickly as possible, put her in her stall, rub her down, put on two blankets, act as if nothing had happened and hope for the best. In the meantime he would go to the treasurer's office, collect the money from the cattle exhibit and pay off the bets. The Fair was over.

For several days we carried water to Gyp and then turned her in the pasture. After a couple of weeks she was again her normal self, a gentle, well- behaved, dependable driving mare—providing no one tried to push her too hard. We never raced her again.

Flax Harvest

In spite of our financial flop at the fair we did quite well for the season. Our ten acres of flax produced an unbelievable yield of twenty-two bushels per acre. The market price was around five dollars a bushel. We saved enough seed for a bigger field the next year, sold the rest, divided the money, and deposited it in our separate bank accounts, to be used wisely as needed and, of course, with the approval of Father and Mother. It was agreed, however, that we deserved a splurge as a starter. First we were going to buy Olga a present but could not think of what to get so gave her the money to spend for what she wanted. Then George bought a larger Eastman Kodak and equipment and supplies for developing pictures, a hobby he had recently acquired. I was in a rut, it seems, and sent for a saddle I had admired in the catalogue for some time. I now had three.

Second Year in Bird Island

Shortly after the fair George and I began our second year of school at Bird Island. He jogged and I rode. This was his Senior year with the winter passing quickly and pleasantly as had the one before. The only special events of the school year I remember are the Senior class play, in which the whole school had as much to do in preparing the stage and scenery and selling tickets as did the class itself, and the graduation. George immediately made plans to enroll in a course in Animal Husbandry at the Agricultural College of the University of Minnesota at St. Paul in September.

Our first job was getting ready to sow our field of flax. We had been able to get most of the plowing done in the Fall so it was not long before we had eighty acres seeded. This would really be something compared to the little patch of ten acres the year before. It grew green and tall as had the previous crop. When in blossom it became a blue lake—a lake of gold, if there ever was such a thing. Then the blooms began to fade and were replaced by millions of small green bulbs that would soon develop into seed-filled pods.

We often multiplied eighty acres by twenty two and then by five and it always came out such a huge sum of money that figuring how to spend it defied all imagination. George, of course, was going away to school and, to begin with, could use an automobile. My thoughts did not go that far but—with a one-track mind—I would first buy a Collins saddle which, in the parlance of today, would be classed as the "Cadillac" of saddles. I might even take the train to Denver, where they were made, during the Christmas vacation and pick one out. There was no limit to what we thought and planned.

Then one morning in August, our field did not glisten as it usually did when the dew reflected the sun. Instead, the reflection was from a great, white sheet of frost. As the sun rose higher, it turned black and in a few days more became a dirty, brownish-green field of nothing but trouble. It had to be gotten rid of because frozen flax was often a source of prussic acid which was about as fast and fatal a poison as was known and, as such, a great danger to livestock. The tough, fibrous stems would not rot down as would the straw of other corps and the stand was so heavy that it could not be plowed under.

It looked as if we would have to harvest and then burn it but as it dried we set it on fire one windy afternoon and stood back as the blaze swept across the field. The bitter smoke irritated our noses and eyes so it was not surprising that a few tears ran down our cheeks as we tried to joke about our eight thousand dollar bonfire.

But our troubles were not over yet. In a couple of days there were wisps of smoke coming up in different places over the field which, we soon discovered were from fires in the peat soil of the old lake bottom. Digging only seemed to spread them so we began hauling water in barrels to drown them out. In some we were successful but others might seem dead only to pop up in four or five days at a distance of thirty or forty feet in one direction or another. It took the heavy Spring rains to quench them all. In the meantime the air for miles around was permeated with the pungent odor of burning peat. Neighbors who had come from places in Europe where peat was used for fuel said the smell reminded them of home. If their memories were happy they were the only pleasant things that came from our great flax fiasco. The field grew wonderful crops of barley and oats the following years, but we were careful not to burn any leftover piles of straw in the next two years of our stay, and there were no instances of unseasonable frost either.

Bill

Some months after we became settled at Bird Island, a young, unmarried and recently ordained minister came to serve the church in town and another in the country. He was much different from the ministers I had known in that he did not preach about fire and brimstone and the Vengeance of the Lord and seemed to believe a happy and smiling spirit was as welcome, if not more so, as one that was sad and gloomy. His daily life must have been based upon this belief since he was always cheerful, friendly, and ready for fun. With much success he led mid-week singfests and organized parties for younger people. He loved games, and if tricks were played he was just as happy to be caught as not. In every way we thought of him as the best. If he understood sex I do not know but he definitely did not recognize its existence in animals—or in horses anyway. He named his driving mare 'Bill' and referred to all horses as "boy."

After a year or so, he planned to go back east for a visit and, as was expected, Father offered to keep Bill for him. So, one evening on the way home from school I stopped by for her. He pleased me by admiring my saddle and more so by asking if I thought I could break Bill to ride in the few weeks he would be away. Instead of turning her in the pasture as we had intended, I kept her in the barn so as to work with her in the evenings.

One day George and I noticed she was in heat and began talking of what a joke it would be if Bill should have a colt. The more we talked, the better the joke sounded so we led the stallion out and took care of the situation. There was no problem since this was our regular chore with our own brood mares and with those of the neighbors who brought them over for that purpose. The only thing we did not do was to record it in the book.

As time went on, our big joke was overshadowed by other events but back in my mind I thought of it, especially when George left to attend the University. By the time he came home for Christmas, Bill was filling out considerably. The minister noticed it and asked Father if it was probable he was over feeding him since he was getting so fat. I do not know the reply he received but am sure Father knew what had taken place. At the Easter vacation Bill was so broad she could hardly get between the buggy shafts. Something was bound to happen soon. As George again left for school he said he wished he could stay for the fun. I wished he could, too, and that I could take my enjoyment from St. Paul, a hundred miles away.

A week or two later as the family, consisting of Father, Mother, a visiting schoolteacher, two hired men, and myself, was sitting down for Sunday dinner the telephone rang. Mother answered and called Father, saying it was the minister. By then there was no more surprise to anyone and the gist of Father's end of the conversation pretty well told the story. It was that Fred would be in very soon with a horse he could use and would partition off some kind of a box stall for Bill and the new colt.

68

Then, before I could suggest old John as the best horse to take, he said to put a halter on Gyp, lead her to town, hitch her to the buggy and acquaint the minister with some of her peculiarities since he probably would be driving her for the next four of five months. If I had been given a chance, I could have put up a tough argument right then but his next two remarks—which, I am sure, he had been thinking of for some time—ended my thoughts along that line. They were to remind the Reverend not to enter Gyp in any horse races and to feed her carefully so she would not get fat like Bill had.

With that I left, the most pleasant prospect in my immediate future being that I could enjoy a cold dinner by myself in a couple of hours more than a hot meal then. When I got to town the minister was standing at the barn door watching with happy amazement as the colt on his long rubbery legs had found the place and was nursing as if he would not have another chance.

A couple of days later I led Bill home with the colt trotting right along. This time I turned her in the pasture where she stayed until it was time to wean the colt. It ran with our horses for the next two years and was sold at our auction sale. The amount it brought was turned over to the minister.

There is no moral to this story but the old adage of, "He who laughs last laughs best," should apply, especially since it involves a fun-loving parson.

Neighbors and Friends

The driveway that led from the public road near town, past our buildings to the road a half a mile east was no more than a hard-packed track along the edge of the field. For one day each year, we posted a sign designating it as a "Private Road" so that, at some future date, the township could not declare it a public highway because of continued use. It was used regularly by the Neibauers, our neighbors on the east, since it saved them nearly a mile on their way to town. They were good neighbors with always a friendly greeting as they passed by. In the winter we were often aroused by the sound of voices and sleigh bells as they drove to Early Mass in the hours long before daylight. During harvest they also attended church early in the morning so as to return home in time to put in a fair day's work in the field.

This practice did not disturb Father although he was firmly against working on Sundays. He said Sunday was a day for rest and work done on that day would be wasted. Occasionally George and I would report having seen the Neibauer harvesting crew, which consisted of the father, three teenage daughters, and a younger son, drinking beer in the field. I am sure Mother considered the beer a greater sin than working on Sunday.

When their oldest daughter was married, we were invited and all went over in the evening to the wedding party. A dance floor had been built, tables loaded with food set up, an orchestra was going full blast, and two bartenders were busy serving drinks. It was a party to be remembered. Until daylight, buggies, and an occasional car, passed our house on the way to town and beyond with people on their way home. At breakfast we teased mother by wondering how she could explain her attendance at such a party to her W.C.T.U. members. In the same vein she replied that she did not know but thought she probably should have caught a ride with some of the revelers in time for Early Mass and stayed for Confession too.

Religious beliefs and customs, however, had no bearing on Father's and Mother's choice of friends. At the other end of our road, on the way to town, lived the Riedners. They were Catholics also, as were most of our neighbors, with a daughter who was a Nun and a son who was studying for the Priesthood. A close friendship developed and lasted the rest of their lives. Years later Father, Mother, and Olga would sometimes visit them over weekends and the son, who had a parish in California, often spent the night with the folks on his way home for a visit.

Haircuts

Another incident which is of no importance and less interest keeps coming to my mind so I shall tell it to describe life on the farm in a minor detail. One Saturday evening, as we often did, George and I with two hired men, Al and Elmer, walked in to town for no reason except that it was Saturday. As we passed the barber shop we suddenly decided to all have our hair clipped to the scalp. On the way home we carried our hats so as to enjoy the cool breeze on our bare heads as we talked of the surprise to the folks in the morning. The surprise fell kind of flat. Apparently Father had seen us clowning around while doing our early morning chores and had gone to the house to prepare Mother for the sight. From there she took over.

Mother greeted us as expected for that time of day as we filed, rather hurriedly, through the kitchen where she was working over the range. When we were seated at the table Father, trying hard to keep a normal voice, asked what we had done in town the evening before. Elmer finally said he had bought a pair of gloves and George continued by describing a set of harness for sale at Hurley's. Silence followed during which a tension built up in me until I blurted that we had all had our hair cut. With a deadpan expression that would have been the envy of a poker player, Mother said she was glad we had thought of it because she noticed that we were all becoming rather shaggy and now we would all be neat and trim for the song festival at church which we planned to attend. There was nothing, she added, to top off a pressed suit, clean hands, and polished shoes like a nice haircut. She then changed the subject while the four of us tried to pull our heads down between shoulder blades as we finished our breakfast. Father could not quite hold in a chuckle as we left for outdoors to pull our hats as far over our ears as possible and began the wait until our hair grew out again.

It did not turn out too bad though. After others became used to our appearance, we agreed this was the best way to wear hair in the summer and promised that next year we would do the same. I doubt if any of us did.

Hired Men

Much could be written about the many hired men we employed over the four years, especially those who hired on for the season or maybe a year. Most were hard working, clean living young men who became almost a part of the family, glad to share our problems and pleased that we shared theirs. Occasionally, however, a loner came along. Smith was one of these. He was a man about forty years old, rather small but tremendously strong. I remember seeing him come in from a field he had finished seeding. He was sitting on the seat of the grain drill with his feet hooked under a brace for support. With his right hand he was driving the four horses while with his left he was pulling a heavy farm wagon.

He was asked for a given name or initials when he first came but said he preferred "Smith" and nothing more. He resented the use of "Mister" as well as a nickname. One friendly fellow worker once called him "Smitty" but did not try it a second time. During his stay of many months, he never mentioned places he had been, work he had done, or things he had seen. He was not really unfriendly in that he would talk about the day's work and the plans for the next day or week without restraint, but he volunteered nothing about his past or his plans for the future. When he left we had the memory of a real good worker and a few canceled checks endorsed by "Smith."

Charlie Shelby was different sort entirely. He was well over six feet tall and as thin as a rail. He was a fair worker with no claim to being overly bright, but at times he showed that he had been thinking. One of these was when he asked Father what his chances would be to marry Olga when she graduated from her medical course and set up a practice. He explained that he could take care of the yard and the stable as well as to drive for her on night calls when the weather and roads were bad. He would be especially good at this because he had the faculty of being able to catch up on lost sleep by napping anywhere and any time the next day. Father already knew this. Apparently Charlie received little encouragement since he did not begin courting. At the end of the season he left for parts unknown but probably ready to dream some more.

George and Horses

George's favorite study, in his course at the University, was "Breeds and Breeding." This, as the name implies, deals with the characteristics of the different breeds of livestock, the part environment had to do with their development, and their improvement by the careful selection of breeding stock. His knowledge of the subject and a flair for detail soon won him a permanent place on the livestock judging team. At the time the Spring term ended, he had found work for the Summer on a farm at Monticello, Minnesota, called Hurdcroft, which raised purebred horses, with the promise he would be one of the attendants who would accompany the show animals on the circuit of Midwest fairs. He knew that the training he would receive and the chance to observe expert judges in the show rings and the probability of meeting and talking to many of them would be very much worth his while.

There were, of course, horse shows of pleasure horses as there still are today, but they were secondary to those of the heavy draft animals. The draft breeds were divided between the black or grey Percherons that originated in France, the bay or sorel Belgians, the huge dark bay or nearly black Shires from England, with their bushy "feathered" legs, and their lighter colored cousins, the Clydesdales from Scotland. Percherons were raised at Hurdcroft.

Father and Mother were in full agreement with George's idea in the belief that the experience he would gain would be worth much more than the wage of an extra man for the three summer months. They had another reason also, which was never voiced in exact words. It was that with his prolonged absence I would continue, as I had for some time, to assume more responsibility and not take the easy way of turning the decisions over to George. Whether I fulfilled their expectations or not was never voiced in exact words either, but I do know we accomplished a great deal during the next two years with a minimum of friction.

Visit to George in Monticello, Minnesota

After two or three weeks, George wrote to suggest that I visit him for a couple of days, including the Fourth of July. I welcomed the trip and so on the designated day left on the early morning train for Minneapolis, with plenty of time for breakfast before boarding the train for Monticello, and arrived around noon where George met me with a horse and buggy for the ride to the farm a mile or two from town.

It was a treat to walk into that great showy barn with stalls of polished oak with brass nameplates and trophies of previous years on display in neat arrangement. There is no way to describe the many perfectly groomed animals that filled the stalls. The activity at the time was the preparation for the coming six-week trip on the fair circuit. Chests were filled with blankets, halters, bridles, grooming equipment, and everything and anything that might be needed by twenty-five or thirty horses that were accustomed to the very best. There were folding cots and blankets for the men who, for this month and a half, would sleep in show barns at the state fairs or in railroad cars rattling along from fair to fair. Some of the older men would recall incidents of other years at Indianapolis or Topeka and mention names of people and horses of importance as if they were as commonplace as a next door neighbor. It sounded like adventure, and I was glad to see that these people accepted George as one of their own. I knew he would make out real well.

A happening one evening would fit well in the memory of an Antique Car buff. It interested me more in later hears than at the time. In the evening, as we sat in the yard at the farmhouse, the chauffeur came down from the family home, said he was going to town to mail a letter, and invited us along for a ride. He was driving a Pierce-Arrow touring car, with brass trimmings from the long gear shift and brake levers on the outside of the body to the rims on the gas- burning headlights that looked as big as water buckets. The upholstery was of glove soft leather and very comfortable. He told us he had been in Europe four times with this car and expected to go again the next summer. In the meantime he would give it a complete overhaul. It must have been at least five years old, which indicates there were some pretty good cars built by 1907.

On the way home I had an assignment that loomed larger than it actually was. I was to pick up a trunk one of our hired men had in storage in Minneapolis and check it as baggage on my railroad ticket. With quite a bit of time between trains, I sized up the eight or ten rickety express wagons and decrepit horses lined up beside the depot. There being little choice between any drivers, I made a deal with the first one. Rather than turn my claim check and the storage charge over to him, and then stand around and wonder if he would return, I got on the seat with him. I was glad he was driving because, even among all those strangers, I would have hated to have been seen driving such a rig. He turned out to be a helpful sort of fellow, though, who knew just where to go to get the trunk and the right express dock at the depot to unload it. When I saw it lifted from the baggage car at Bird Island, I had a certain feeling of accomplishment. I felt that I had a pleasant, interesting, and somewhat educational outing. I was ready now to begin preparing for harvest.

Harvest

Because of a rainy spell during seeding time, the last part of the crop was not ripening early as usual. So, as we readied the machinery for harvest, we decided to begin cutting with one binder instead of two as we had done the other years. This went well but soon it became apparent the operations would have to be speeded up. I suggested, since we had a good start, to continue with one binder but change horses so as to put in longer days. Father agreed to keep the horses ready as long as I wanted to ride the binder.

So, for the next two to three weeks, I began each day at six o'clock with five horses pulling a binder around and around a field. At about eleven Father would bring out another team to use until four o'clock. Then the first team would take over until dark. The next day the horses that had had the two shifts would work only one so I had fresh and well rested animals all the time.

At first this seemed a kind of fun. Then it became a sort of an endurance contest and real tiring work. At the age of seventeen, however, weariness can be easily overcome with a hearty supper and a few hours sleep. By the time the job was done I had, by rough calculation, ridden that binder seat five hundred and fifty miles and used nearly two hundred miles of twine. This may have been a record but there was no prize except the satisfaction of a good job done. With a good stacking crew, the harvest was soon over, the county fair gone by, and I was back in school beginning my senior year.

Fred's brother, George Hansen, about 1917

Railroad Grading Workers

During the years we were at Bird Island the Milwaukee railroad was adding a track to the one which intersected our farm from the southeast to the northwest, so as to have a double track line from Minneapolis to the west. The grading was all done by horse and mule drawn equipment, operating from a camp of tents that moved a few miles at a time as the work progressed. With the completion of a section of twenty some miles of grading, a gang of over two hundred tie and rail laying laborers arrived in a long row of bunk cars and set up their residence on a siding east of town and just across the road from one of our fields.

These men were of dark complexion and sturdy build. Most of them had heavy mustaches. They wore heavy woolen clothing, even in the heat of Summer, and had the appearance of wearing several pairs of pants. It was said they were Croatians or Serbians or whatever related name came to mind. We had a waving acquaintance with two or three of the camp attendants. Otherwise they kept very much to themselves except on Sundays when, in groups of five or six, they would travel for miles in every direction on foraging expeditions trying to buy animals for food.

In spite of a lack of knowledge of the language, they were shrewd bargainers and understood the value of money. Their choice was any edible animal small enough that it could be consumed in one day. These included everything from chickens to pigs, sheep, and calves. Transportation was simple. As an animal was purchased its legs were trussed together, a long ash pole was inserted between them and carried on the shoulders of two men. At camp the chickens were placed in cages but the others were tethered to stakes and cared for until used.

Some of our neighbors, some of whom had been immigrants themselves, mistrusted these people and felt there should be laws to prevent such foreigners from roaming the country side but, as far as

I know, there was only one instance in which they were accused, justly or unjustly, of any wrongdoing. A store in town was broken into one night and a couple of dozen men's suits were taken. The sheriff searched the bunk cars but found nothing. Then six or seven weeks later, when we threshed a setting of grain stacks in a field near the camp, the clothes were found on the ground and covered by a few loose bundles. We took them into town but they were wet and moldy and so damaged by mice and crickets as to be worthless. Opinions differed as to whether the clothing was stolen by the railroad workers, who lost their nerve with the search by the sheriff, or by some local person with the same affliction.

Senior Year in High School

With school affairs, basketball games, sleigh rides and parties, the last year of high school passed quickly. No one worried about failing to graduate. There seemed to be an unwritten rule to the effect that anyone who had put in three years at the Bird Island High School was sure of a diploma at the end of the fourth.

A special event during the spring term was the class play. This seemed an unnecessary activity with none of us having any acting ability and none aspiring towards such a career. But it was a thing that had always been done and so, influenced by the coach, we chose *The Taming of the Shrew* for our script. Dressed in outlandish costumes that were supposed to picture those worn in some pre-Shakespearean age, we bumbled through our roles and mumbled words and phrases we did not understand in tones and with accents far removed from those intended by the author. We succeeded in boring the audience to utter distraction.

The class picnic was more fun. Although the faculty knew what was going to happen and gave silent consent, the entire class arose and, without permission and in defiance of all rules, marched from the assembly room. At the City Park we roasted wieners, ate cookies and ice cream, signed autographs, and vowed to keep in touch with each other for the rest of our days.

Then came graduation, with the graduates sweltering under their gowns as the audience squirmed and fanned while the visiting speaker gave the customary oration on the true meaning of "commencement." Graduation was over with the presents ready for use. The four I remember well were a tailor-made suit and a leather suitcase from Father and Mother, a Gillette safety razor in a traveling case from Olga, and an Eastman Kodak from George.

Decisions

For some time there had been family talk about selling the farm. Now, with all of us home for a few days, the subject was discussed thoroughly with the conclusion that with Olga and George both away and my intention of attending a veterinary college, this would be an ideal time. With real estate values having more than doubled in the last four years, the decision was easy to make. This would be the last year.

This summer George had arranged to work on a horse farm at LeMars, Iowa with the same circuit of fairs to be followed as the preceding year. Before he left he told of reserving a room at the Minnesota Hotel on Washington Avenue for the last three days of the State Fair and invited me to join him. I accepted.

The sale of the farm was no problem and by the last of June the deal had been made, with the understanding we would give possession by a certain date in October. The work went smoothly with no concern about Fall plowing or care of the livestock the next winter. Harvest was over by the first of September and during a rainy week I prepared for my appointment with George on the designated day.

Terror during Departure for the State Fair

On a drizzly, drippy morning, Father took me to town in ample time to catch the early train, which came through an hour or so before daylight. Main street was quiet and deserted as we drove its length to the depot at the far end. When we were within a few feet of our destination, a sound, much like two fire crackers exploding in a barrel, came from somewhere beyond the building. It was so startling the horses stopped in their tracks. As they did, I stepped from the buggy as Father made a U turn and went back down the street. I walked to the building and began the scariest and most unforgettable quarter of an hour in my memory.

The depot was the typical long building with the roof flattened out at the eaves and extending to make a protective cover over most of the platform. Under this a few widely spaced lanterns were hung. They gave some light but also accentuated the surrounding darkness. Keeping under this roof I stayed close to the end of the building to the corner. As I turned I collided with the night marshal, who looked as if he had seen a ghost. I was not well acquainted with him but knew he was regarded as a capable officer and a man who did not know the meaning of fear. His appearance disputed this.

Even in the poor light, his face was ashen. In his left hand he held an unlighted flashlight and, in his right, a snub nosed revolver which he pressed against my midriff. Instinctively I grabbed his wrist to push it away and was surprised that he seemed to have no more strength than a small child. In an almost inaudible voice, he asked if I had heard two shots. When I nodded in reply, he indicated I was to come with him and turned back in the direction from which he had come.

I put my bag in the waiting room and followed him past the lighted office, where the station agent was busy with his telegraph keys, to the other end of the building and directly to a box car that loomed in the darkness nearby. As we drew near the car, I heard movement and sounds of moaning or groaning from inside. The marshal, in a hoarse whisper, told me to climb in and tell him what had happened. When I asked for the flashlight, he muttered something about "refusing to help an officer" and emphasized his order by again pressing with the gun. Again I caught his wrist and with my other hand took the light.

The beam showed the car to be empty except for one man who was on his back along the wall and not far from the door. When I came closer I saw he was trying to swing one arm and that blood was spurting from a wound in his chest. He was either moaning or trying to say something. My one thought, which was not based on reason, was that the most urgent thing and my responsibility was to get him out of that car. So with a pull on an arm and another on a leg I managed to move him. As this went on the moaning lessened to a gurgly sound.

By the time I reached the door the gurgle had stopped and the blood was no longer spurting but flowing continued. When the man's feet were protruding from the doorway the marshal asked if I thought he was dead. With my reply that I thought so, he became a changed person, as if this was now something he could understand and take care of. In a nearly normal voice he told me to stay there while he went to the station platform for a baggage truck. With his pulling on the legs and my lifting and pushing on the upper part of the body, we lowered it to the truck and wheeled it to the lighted area in front of the office.

My light-colored raincoat was ruined with blood. As I took it off, the marshal, in a businesslike manner, spread it over the body. The station agent invited me to wash in his private office and, with his help, managed to get most of the blood from my face and shirt. The tip of one coat sleeve, the bottom of one pants leg , and one shoe were badly soaked, but with the free use of water we got most of it out. I asked the marshal if I must stay, but he said it would not be necessary. He would call the sheriff as soon as the train left and since he knew as much about it as I did, one story would be enough. He seemed anxious for me to go. I could understand why he would not welcome a report of his behavior.

On the train I was kept busy telling the story to different passengers and new arrivals. By the time we reached Minneapolis my pants and coat were dry, but they felt uncomfortable. When George met me I proposed buying a new suit and shoes but he had me get a shoe shine at the depot and at the hotel he had a bell boy take my suit to be cleaned. After washing thoroughly and changing clothes, I put on a pair of his pants and we went for breakfast. When we returned to the room my suit was already there. The fair occupied our time for the next two days. Then it was time for him to go back to Iowa with the show horses and for me to return to Bird Island where the murder was the talk of the town.

The victim had been identified as a resident of a neighboring town who had been working in the harvest fields to the west. He had gotten off an east bound freight the afternoon before and had spent the evening drinking in one saloon or the other. He had seemed to enjoy showing a very large roll of bills from time to time and returning them to his inside coat pocket. This had been called to the attention of the marshal. The coroner's verdict was that he had been killed by "a party or parties unknown with robbery as the motive."

Among the stories going around was the one said to have been told by the marshal. He said he had followed the man at closing time, hoping he would not head for the hobo jungle and was relieved when he saw him climb into a car near the depot. He had stayed in the darkness and watched for awhile to be sure he was not molested. He had returned to the car a couple of times between his rounds of duty on Main Street and was pleased each time to find the man asleep and untroubled. Then, shortly before train time, he had heard the sound of two shots while he was on the street a block and a half away. Some special sense told him where the sound came from. He hurried towards the depot where he caught up with me and the two of us removed the body from the car. When the sheriff came they examined the body but found no roll of bills. The boxcar was gone, having been picked up by one of the two freights that met about daylight, and the hobo jungle was deserted, the occupants having left on the same trains.

The story, attributed to the marshal, was not true as it applied to my part in the incident because he did not catch up with me, he could not have run the block and a half in the same time it took me to step from the buggy to the depot and Father had not seen or heard anyone running as he drove back down the street. I blamed these discrepancies on the way stories are changed in the telling and expected the marshal to stop me on the street to, at least, tell what had happened after I left. Even though he might not have been proud of his conduct that morning, I felt he owed me this since we had been in the mess together. It soon became plain he was trying to avoid me—and succeeding—in such ways as suddenly stepping between two buildings or into a store when we approached each other and in a minute or so appearing on the other side of the street. In a way this suited me because, deep down, I am sure I was somewhat afraid of him. It was not long before we had our sale and left.

As time passed, I graduated from the Kansas City Veterinary College, Nina and I were married, I served in the army during World War I, made two or three false starts at establishing a practice and finally settled at Pelican Rapids. In those years I had never been back to Bird Island. However, Father had been there several times on business and he and Mother had kept in touch with friends. So while visiting one time, he told that he had recently learned who shot the transient in the box car on that dreary morning, twelve years or more ago. Before he died the marshal had confessed to the crime. When I heard this, no doubt my knees shook more that they had at the actual time, as I remembered that gun being pushed in my middle.

Of course, the confession is strictly hearsay but it comes so near to what must have happened that I shall report part of it as it was told. The marshal did follow the man to the box car for protection and return two or three times during the night to check on his safety.

On one of these occasions, he had stopped for a cup of coffee and a chat with the depot agent and had told him of the sleeping man. The agent said two freights were to meet at about daybreak with the west bound to pick up as many empty cars as the switching time allowed. No doubt the sleeper would awake to find himself back where he had started from the day before. As the marshal thought of this on his round of the street, he also wondered what would happen if someone bent on robbery made the trip on the same car. He came back to the car again and, as he stood at the door listening to the deep breathing, thought how easy it would be for anyone to climb in, remove the roll of bills and leave without even awakening him. Hardly realizing what he was doing, he found himself with the money in his hand when the sleeper roused, tried to defend himself, and called for help. Afraid of being recognized, the marshal shot him twice. Then he panicked with his only thought to get away from there as quickly as possible. Had he returned to Main Street by the way of an alley and then come back later without saying he had heard the shots, his story would have been believable. Instead, he came by way of the depot platform where we collided. No doubt that roll of bills in his pocket felt as big as a football. Later, when he removed the rubber band, he found the bulk was made up of stage money with a five-dollar bill and a one wrapped around the outside. SIX DOLLARS.

Moving from Bird Island to Minneapolis

Our auction sale was a big one with all the farm machinery fairly new. There were almost a hundred head of horses, from the big iron-gray Percheron stallion down to the spring crop of colts which had just been weaned. George obtained a leave from his classes and came home to help. With his experience with show horses, he braided colored bunting on the manes and tails of some of the best matched teams while I blackened hooves with paint. It was a sale to be remembered. It ended our four years at Bird Island.

84

Epilogue

After leaving Bird Island, Father and Mother moved to an apartment in Minneapolis and kept house for Olga and George. A year or so later they bought a home in St. Paul where they spent the rest of their lives in comfort. Actually, it was in luxury far above anything they could have possibly dreamed when they came to America as immigrants, not so many years before.

Olga and I are the last members of the family who lived at Bird Island, George having died in 1918. Incidentally, the year before he had received one of the highest honors in his field by being chosen as the officiating judge at the International Livestock Show at Chicago.

Olga has retired and lives in Minneapolis after a distinguished career of fifty-five years in the practice of medicine.

Nina and I are enjoying a comfortable retirement in Independence, Missouri, with four of her sisters and one brother as neighbors. Although none of the members of our immediate family, which consists of our son and his wife, their three daughters, and our five great-grand children, live here, we keep in touch and manage to meet from time to time. We are proud of them all.

On March 3rd, 1977 Nina and I will have been married sixty years. We are thankful for all these years together. During that time it seems I have never been able to find the words to tell how much her care and affection have meant to me and how important her understanding and judgment have been. Maybe this is a good time to try.

Independence, Missouri

September 29, 1976

Chapter 3

Two Summers in Armstrong, Iowa,

by Fred Hansen, Sr.

Fred Hansen wrote this description of summers in 1914 and 1916 as a letter to his cousin, John G Thomsen. Fred wanted John G to know more about his father, who had died in 1923 when John G was just two years old. John Thomsen, my grandfather, had emigrated from Denmark the year after his sister, Sophia, and was a practicing veterinary surgeon in the Armstrong area. His first wife, Bina, had died in 1913, and he had hired a new Danish immigrant, Kirstine, to keep house. She and John were married in 1919, and John G was born in 1921. Fred's descriptions here overlap with his writings in "Sixty Years . . . . And More, Part I."

Letter to John G Thomsen

Dear Cousin John,

In this I shall try to tell you some of the things I remember of the time I spent with your parents in Armstrong in 1914 and again in 1916. I shall refer to them as Uncle John and Kirstine, the names by which I knew them. They were not yet married.

Uncle John's wife, my Aunt Bina, had died some time before, and Kirstine was employed as his housekeeper. She had not been in this country very long and was having some language trouble, especially in taking calls from some of the non-Danish clients. Some of her responses and interpretations of messages she had received were both amusing and confusing but she laughed at and profited by her mistakes and was soon doing real well.

Many of the things I remember are of a decidedly humorous nature. By relating these I do not want to give the impressions that life was mostly fun and frivolity. It was not. Uncle John had great pride in his profession and practiced it with diligence and dignity. He was, however, a fun loving man with the ability, and often an urge, to change a commonplace situation into one of spontaneous hilarity. Kirstine also had a sense of humor and was well able to hold her own in that department.

First Extended Visit—1914

It would probably be fitting about now to tell of the events which led to my first visit. My parents had sold their farm and in the fall of 1913 moved to Minneapolis where Olga and George were students at the University. I applied for admission to the Veterinary College in Toronto from which Uncle John had graduated [the Ontario Veterinary College]. Through some quirk of fate my application was temporarily lost in the mail and did not arrive in time for my entrance that year. This was quite a disappointment. The following year, for some unknown reason, I enrolled in the Kansas City Veterinary College instead and continued through to graduation in 1917. Nina and I became acquainted during that time and we were married shortly before graduation. I came home with both a wife and a diploma, a combination not as common then as now. I have always been grateful to the finger of fate which guided my destiny through that period and ever since as well.

After the activity of life on the farm, the idleness of the city became tiring. I attended a business college for a few weeks but could not work up much interest. I was looking for a job of some sort when Uncle John came up to spend Thanksgiving with us. He invited me to visit him after Christmas and thought he could find something for me to do. This was the period during which the use of cholera serum and live virus was coming into full swing in an attempt to check the spread of hog cholera and, as a result, the work of most veterinarians was increasing greatly.

In January of 1914 I arrived in Armstrong and became part of the household which included Uncle John, Kirstine, and Alvilda,[17] who was attending school. I went on country calls with Uncle John and helped in whatever way I could with any chores that came along. To my credit I will say that I was a willing worker and had a knack for handling animals. Usually I could control a stubborn or frightened patient better than the owner could. I soon became familiar with the care and use of instruments and with the preparation and administration of drugs and medicines. The State officials issued me a permit to "vaccinate" swine and before long I was being sent on an occasional call, with, of course, explicit instructions as to the procedure. (I would not recommend this kind of training to anyone who planned to take up "Book Learning" later but that thought, long ago, became as water over the dam.)

Transportation—Motorcycle and Car

With me assigned to more and more individual calls, a problem of transportation arose. To solve it I bought a motorcycle. It was an Excelsior Twin but could be fittingly called Hansen's Folly. There were too many muddy roads for its use to be practical. On top of that it gave me a lot of mechanical trouble and returning to town with it loaded in a farm wagon became an old story. After a couple of months it came to rest in the barn until I sold it a year later.

---

[17] Avilda was Kirstine's younger cousin.

DR. J. THOMSEN, Veterinarian.

John Thomsen, brother of Sophia Hansen, about 1910

Uncle John's car at that time was an Imperial Roadster.[18] It was big and strong and flashy. With its full leather upholstery, with the brass-wear polished, and the exhaust sounding in perfect sequence, it was an impressive vehicle. On a gravel road, at dusk, it was really spectacular. It had a pair—the only ones I have ever seen—of steel studded leather outer tires which would send a shower of sparks remindful of twin comets.

The car did have a few weak points, too. The most serious of these was the almost and sometimes total lack of braking power. There were brake shoes only on the rear wheels and they fitted outside of the drum, subjecting them to slush and mud and dust. The only time they really would hold was on a cold winter morning when the shoes would be frozen to the drums. If crawling underneath and tapping with a hammer did not loosen them a bucket of hot water

---

[18] This was actually an Imperial "44-6" model made by the Imperial Automobile Company in Jackson, Michigan. Imperial Roadsters were made by the Chrysler Corporation between 1931 and 1933.

usually would.

Behind the wheel of the Imperial, Uncle John could be likened to a knight of old, mounted on a fiery, half-tamed charger and ready to accept any challenge or to offer a few of his own. At a time when the expression, "Forty miles an hour" denoted an unbelievable highway speed, he did not hesitate to drive the speedometer needle to the top figure of 60 and push it some on the second go 'round. It was not unusual to see him pass up a farm driveway and then battle the car to a halt a quarter of a mile beyond. There were probably some who described Thomsen as a reckless driver. On this I shall not comment but shall only add that to enjoy the ride, his passenger needed a streak of recklessness of his own.

You will remember that the garage at the end of the driveway was on an elevation of two or three feet. The most practical way to park was to stop at the foot of the incline, shift to low gear, drive in slowly, and then quickly turn off the ignition. He enjoyed trying to go in in high gear and succeeded just often enough to make it worth a try again. Usually he went right through into a garden whose owner I do not remember. He promptly paid the damage and I imagine she had the most profitable garden in the town. This happened so many times that he put hinges on the back doors, reinforcements for the car springs, and light springs for the latch.

The Ford which replaced the Imperial did not give him much of a thrill. He drove it moderately but with no affection and when we went together, I was always the driver.

The problem of a second car was never really worked out. The Ford dealer – Mr. Gibbs, I believe – could sell Fords faster than he could get them in. He liked to have a car "broken in" before turning it over to a purchaser. By some arrangement, I drove most of these new cars a few miles or part or all of a day before he delivered them. At times he would lend me an old one that had been taken in on a trade. At other times a farmer would come in and get me and bring me back when the work was done. And there was always Lee Olson.

Lee Olson

Lee drove an auto livery. It was said that his order at the gas pump was for five gallons of gas, a quart of oil, and two quarts of whiskey. Presumably the pump operator was also the bootlegger. Although I rode many times with Lee, I never learned much about him since he was never sober enough to carry on a conversation. He knew every farm road, though, and could guide his Model T Ford around mud holes and over short cuts with remarkable skill.

When we arrived at our destination, he would take a little nip and prepare to relax while I went about the business for which we had come. When ready to leave I would crank the car while he took a good sized slug from his bottle and pound the cork home as an indication that he was well enough fortified to make it to the next stop, and away we would go. Like all of us, he had shortcomings but he had good points too. He was a good driver, he never gossiped, and he never drank while driving.

Stories from Practice—Lost Money

Since many of the things I remember are of unrelated events, it might be a good idea to separate these stories, as I have above, with little regard for continuity or sequence.

Saturday was the stay-at-home day with farmers bringing a variety of animals for treatments. Monday we went to Ringsted where a part of the livery barn was set aside for the same purpose. Wednesday was the day for Swea City where Uncle John had a small building of his own, not far from the depot and which we called "the Shack." When the roads were bad, which was often, we would use the train which went east in the morning and came back in the afternoon.

When we arrived in Swea City, Uncle John would usually think of an errand at the drug store while I opened the Shack, built a fire, and got ready for the day's business. About a half an hour before train time in the afternoon, he would leave me to clean up and take our equipment to the depot. He never missed the train but came quite close many times.

On one occasion I looked at my watch after the train was in motion and discovered, to my dismay, that I had lost two five-dollar bills that had been folded up in my watch pocket. I felt bad about it but he kept assuring me the money had be to on the floor of the Shack. The next Wednesday he took one bag from the depot and headed directly for the Shack to prove that he was right and handed me what he had found—a ten dollar bill. I hunted carefully around the building and along the path but never found my two fives.

Kirstine Mishaps

One night in early summer we had a storm with enough wind to bring down a few tree branches which in turn broke the power line leading to the house. The next morning Uncle John and I went out and picked up the scatterings with little attention to the wire. If someone had suggested that we be careful of it we would probably have wondered what he meant. Live wires were not common in Armstrong. He had called the light plant and been told that someone would be along and fix it soon.

About that time Kirstine came out with a clothes line which she customarily fastened between the trees for the laundry. The wire was in her way so she picked it up with the intention of moving it to the side. Instead, she moved in the most spectacular manner—straight up and then flat on her bottom with her legs and feet extended. For some reason people often react to such a sight with an involuntary laugh even though they know that the incident is not a laughing matter. I guess we were guilty. She next pivoted around with her legs still stretched out and said, "I like it NOT." That became a byword around the house for a while and our family still uses it once in a while.

She had another accident a couple of years later at which no one laughed. She wanted to learn to drive the Model T Ford and so one Sunday morning I gave her lesson number one, which went real well. After dinner I was writing a letter in the office when she came by and suggested a second ride. I agreed and said I was just about done with the letter and we could mail it on the way past the post office. A minute later there was the sound of the car back firing and a muffled scream. Uncle John and I were in the yard in nothing flat and found that she had tried to crank the motor without retarding the spark. Instead of the crank pulling from her grasp and coming around just in time to break the arm above the wrist—as usually happened—it had pulled her body forward so that she came down with her face on the radiator cap. It was pretty bad with, as I remember, four teeth either broken or gone. The rest of that afternoon was divided between the doctor, the dentist, and cold packs but it was not long before she went at driving again and became good at it.

Stringberries

I think Henry Brooks kept the house supplied with vegetables since I do not remember any garden except Uncle John's strawberries. I do not know when he set out the plants but I remember how he fertilized, hoed, and watered them faithfully with the promise that there would be berries for all by the Fourth of July. He anticipated that, being of the ever-bearing variety, they would easily produce until fall. As time went on, they grew like weeds but with never a sign of a berry or even a blossom. He stood firm on his promised date, however, even when the third of July arrived with no change.

On the morning of the Fourth he arose quite early and explained to me that he was going to work a little before breakfast. I thought he meant in the office and so went back to sleep. Shortly before breakfast he came in with a dish of beautiful strawberries and said there were still a few green ones left on the vines to be picked later.

It did not take much study to find that they were attached with thread. We joked him quite awhile about his stringberries.

This name goes back to a somewhat similar incident of several years before. When I was about four years old[19] my mother and I visited Aunt Bina and Uncle John for a few days. Although I remember some incidents of the visit this story was probably impressed upon my memory by its being retold so many times. He had a couple of small trees near the barn which he said would someday have apples hanging from the branches and that they could be brought down by shaking the trunk. Since I knew apples came in barrels, I was not taken in by this story at all. But one day he called us out and, sure enough, there were ten or twelve apples hanging on the trees. He told me to close my eyes and shake as hard as I could. I learned later that at the same time he rolled a couple from his pocket to the ground and had arranged four or five supposedly trick knots that would release apples from the tree with the jerk of a string. Something went wrong and as I opened my eyes the first thing I saw was an apple suspended from a branch by about eight inches of string. It was often told that I said, "I think they are string apples," a judgment and remark of which I am still rather proud.

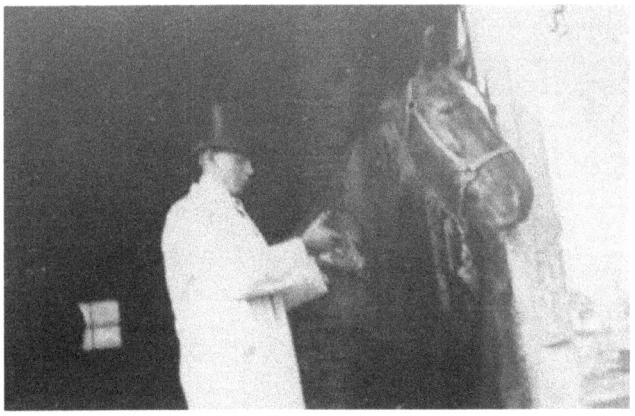

Fred Hansen Sr. caring for John Thomsen's horse, Lucy. 1916.

---

[19] About 1899.

Fun with the Horses—Lucy and Polly

Lucy's mate was Polly. She was probably so named because of a slight deformity with which she was born. Her upper jaw projected over the lower so that the incisors did not meet properly. This condition was not unusual and was known as "Parrot Mouth." It was worth any one's time to see this team hitched to the buggy, which was in place in the driveway of the barn. First the gates of the stalls would be unlocked and Lucy's harness taken from the pegs and held in place. At a signal she would open the gate, walk into the harness and then stand perfectly still until it was buckled. Then she would go to the buggy and take her proper place. Then Polly would do the same and both patiently await the completion of the job. The first year I was in Armstrong I drove them quite a bit—for exercise if nothing else.

One afternoon, while Kirstine was downtown, a call came in for us to go to the country. As we loaded into the Ford one of the horses in the barn whinnied. Uncle John said something about horses never having much fun and so we led them both into the kitchen and tied them to the kitchen range. When we came home both horses were back in their stalls. For some reason we found things to do outside until Kirstine called us to supper. Nothing was said about horses in the kitchen then or at any time later.

A couple of weeks later we had a trip to make in the middle of the night. When we returned a couple of hours later, we took our shoes off in the office so as to make as little noise as possible and went in our stocking feet to the bedroom. In the dining room we bumped into Lucy and Polly, tied to the foot of his bed and presumably wondering what people would think of next. They were even standing on stable blankets that had been brought from the barn. At breakfast time nothing was said about horses in the bedroom or at any time later.

Fred's Motorcycle Gets Stuck on a Train Track

The longest and most memorable trip on my motorcycle was to Buffalo Center where I was to be met by a farmer who would take me out to vaccinate some calves against black leg. Everything went well until some miles past Swea City when the road, such as it was, suddenly ended in a sea of impassable mud. That would have been a good place to turn around and go home but instead I backtracked to a crossroad and went the rest of the way on the railroad track that paralleled the road. With the exception of having to get over the cattle guards and a couple of narrow culverts, I did quite well on the path at the ends of the ties for several miles. When I arrived at the designated meeting place there were four or five men sitting on the platform in front of the store. They were interested in the motorcycle and asked where I had come from. When I told them Armstrong, one of them became downright mean. He knew that no vehicle with wheels could come over that road and wanted to bet five dollars on it. I did not want to bet but did explain that I had come part of the way on the railroad. His friends told him that on the strength of that he should pay me the money and learn to keep his mouth shut. They were still giving him a bad time when the farmer drove up and I left.

The loafers were gone when I got on the motorcycle in the afternoon and began to retrace my route of the morning. About halfway on the railroad section the motor suddenly backfired and died. This had happened before and once in a while I had been able to remedy the trouble with a judicious tap on the carburetor and a gentle turn on the needle valve. When I opened the tool kit I was surprised to find a five dollar bill. Loud Mouth had paid up.

No twisting or turning would start the motor and I soon realized I was utterly stalled. The thought that had been in the back of my mind all day came boldly forward and proclaimed that I should have taken the train instead of the motorcycle in the first place. About that time I heard the whistle of the afternoon train heading for Armstrong and points beyond. As it came into sight I began to wave and the engineer began to blow his whistle as if to scare me off the track. He had just about succeeded when the train slowed down and finally came to a stop.

The members of the train crew were not a bit happy at what I had done and it sounded as if trespassing on railroad property and stopping a scheduled train at an unauthorized place were lesser crimes than those of which I was actually guilty. They made it sound as if prison would be a blessing. But they knew me somewhat from the weekly trips to Swea City and realized I was in pretty bad trouble. They finally accepted my argument, in which I was upheld by many of the passengers, that since the train was now stopped it would not help the situation to pull away and leve me stranded. One passenger came to my aid by pointing out that if I had flagged the train down because of a broken rail I would be a hero suddenly everyone seemed to become happy. There were not enough handholds on the motorcycle for all the help I had in loading in on the baggage car. I arrived home neither triumphant nor defeated, but with enough battle scars to last me for the day.

John Is Sniffed Out

One day in early spring we went to a town on past Buffalo Center to test a herd of cattle for tuberculosis. We went by train in the morning with the plan that Uncle John would get me started and then come home on the afternoon train. I would stay overnight, complete the test, and return the next day. At noon we ate at a restaurant or rooming house that was run by a coarse-looking woman with a voice and vocabulary to match her appearance. Besides smaller tables for transients there was a long table for a dozen or so employees of the farm who were at that season cleaning feed lots and spreading the manure on the fields. As we were through eating the woman tapped Uncle John on the shoulder and called him to the phone. After talking he thanked her and asked how she had known who to call to the phone. "It was easy," she said. "When I heard they wanted to talk to a horse doctor I smelled you out with no trouble, even in this bunch of 'turd' tossers." This was one of the few times he seemed to be without a fitting reply. He had one, I am sure, because when we reached the street he explained to me what a mouth wash and body wash with a cresol solution would do for that woman but it did not seem prudent to return to tell her so.

John Makes a Faux Pas

Another incident when words were hard to come by occurred at the farm of John Thompson where, one noon, we had been asked in for dinner. Mrs. Thompson had a name as a jelly and jam maker, and preserves of all kinds were her specialty. When the meal was nearly over, she remarked that she hoped the small dish of some certain preserve had been enough so that everyone had, at least, a small helping and then asked Uncle John if he had enjoyed it. Indeed he had, he said, and went on in a complimentary manner that she need not apologize for the small helpings since the best of things came in small amounts, when it suddenly dawned on him—as everyone else at the table already knew— he had mistaken the dish for an individual dish of sauce and had eaten it all.

Beer Runs to Minnesota

Even though Uncle John occasionally relished a little nip on a cold winter morning and now and then a long cool drink on a hot summer evening and once in a while a bottle of beer with his supper, no one could consider him a drinking man. But with even a slight drain on the supply it was necessary from time to time to replenish it by making a trip to Ceylon, Minnesota, since Iowa, or at least Emmet County, was dry.

These were fun trips with Uncle John at his jovial best and with his imagination on free rein. I remember our main harmless joke was figuring ways to foil the imaginary minions of the law who were supposed to be lurking everywhere. One ruse that never failed was to leave the saloon in the opposite direction from which we had arrived and to mention such names as New Ulm or Mankato and after a block or so circle around and head for home. The bottled goods were placed in wet grain sacks which, of course, had to be handled carefully. There were reasons for this. The wet sacks helped to keep the beer cold, the appearance could lead an officer to believe we had a sack of fish, and nosy neighbors would get less satisfaction from a gift of roasting ears than from a case of beer being carried into the house.

One afternoon on the way home from Ceylon we stopped in the shade to split a bottle of beer. By tacit understanding a glass or half bottle of beer was the limit of my alcoholic indulgence, either on such a trip or at home. But anything out of a bottle was strong drink to me who had signed the pledge at a tender age, had been a member of the Loyal Temperance Legion, and whose mother was the personification of the W.C.T.U and wore a brooch in the shape of Carrie Nation's hatchet as an emblem of her loyalty to the principles of total and utter Prohibition. As we sat and drank, Uncle John suddenly said, "I wonder what Sophie would do if she came along about now." He thought a minute and continued, "I know what she would do. She would skin me alive with that little hatchet she always wears." I believe he was right.

To me it seems Pete Smith[20] was Uncle John's closest friend. He was also an able straight man for any drollery that came to mind and could pick up his cues with ease. This story had to do with such an instance. Part of it came out bit by bit after the dust settled, and I shall tell it as best I can.

One Saturday evening these two set out in the new Buick on a "bootleg" run to Ceylon. The Buick was a good car in every way except for one fault which, I guess, has not been corrected to this day. The accelerator, which we called the gas pedal, was placed in the very same spot on the floor as the brake pedal of the Ford.

---

[20] Peter Smith, also a Danish immigrant about the same age as John, farmed just south of Armstrong.

Anyway, as they came in the saloon, they realized something big was afoot, with more of the imaginary spies and revenuers around than usual. So they became a little crafty on their own and addressed each other as Pat and Mike. After loading the contraband in the car, they came back in for a beer and to learn whatever they could. They both distinctly heard words being sent out to the patrol to be on the lookout for a couple of Irishers who would be heading towards Dolliver. To give this plan ample time they had another beer and then came on home without mishap—that is almost. As he turned to the left at the end of the driveway Uncle John realized he was going a little faster than he had planned. This posed no real problem. He would merely step heavily on the brake and come to a stop in a cloud of dust between the house and the barn. That is where this defect in design came into play and instead of stepping heavily on the brake, he stepped heavily on the gas pedal and the car came to a stop in a cloud of dust, twigs, leaves and broken clothes lines and wedged between the trees. It was found that little damage was done, with only a scraped fender and some bark from a tree, so they began to unload. Pete Smith had some trouble getting his sack out because there was little room to open the door. He finally succeeded but as he turned, he caught his toe and sat down flat with his sack hitting the walk with a crash that sounded as if all the bottles were broken. At the same time Uncle John came around the back of the car with his load and in an attempt to avoid stepping on Pete lost his balance and sat down beside him with the same sound of shattering glass. Surprisingly few bottles were broken but, at the moment, Pat and Mike were pretty well subdued and could have been easily apprehended by any secret agent, even an imaginary one.

Gadgets—Car Extractor

Uncle John loved gadgets and when an advertisement came showing a well-dressed man turning a handle on a contraption and pulling a well stuck car out of a mud hole, he lost no time in sending for it. We did wonder how he got from the car to the dry ground without his shoes being muddy but gave it little serious thought.

The package came on a Saturday so on Sunday afternoon we set out to try it. There was a pretty good mud hole a half mile or so south of town with, on one side, a fairly solid lane. I drove carefully on this with the intention of gradually creeping in with a sort of tip-toe action. Suddenly he reached over and gave the steering wheel a turn and at the same time pulled down on the gas lever and there we were in hub deep mud. We got the gadget from the back seat, hooked onto the front axle, strung the cable to dry ground, drove in the inter-supporting stakes and began turning the crank. Nothing happened. There was little room for us both to get a hold on the handle but by combining our strength as best we could we managed to pull the stakes from the ground. We reset them and I got in the seat to drive while he cranked. The result of this was that we kept miring down deeper. With no more ado he unhooked and carefully wound up the cable, tossed it into the deepest part of the mud hole, and stood on it until it sank. I suggested returning it and getting his money back but he explained that anyone gullible enough to fall for the picture on the advertisement and stupid enough to deliberately turn a car into a deep mud hole on a Sunday afternoon would have no chance with that bunch of slickers. We walked on to Pete Smith's for a team to pull us out.

Telephone

An instrument that had advanced from the novelty stage to one of dependability, long before my arrival at Armstrong, was the extension telephone. You may remember it. It could be used for incoming calls only unless someone went to the office and rang central. It was meant for night calls and hung on a hook beside the bed. However, so many farmers called at mealtimes that the cord was lengthened and another hook placed beneath the dining room table. Some of the conversations carried on during meals and the frankness of the discussions might have been disturbing to a close adherent to the rules of table etiquette—or to someone with a queasy stomach, for that matter—but this was all in the day's work and this telephone served its purpose well.

Operating Table

If the huge equine operating table was still in existence when you were a child, you are bound to remember it. I do not know when it was purchased and installed but it must have been almost too expensive to be considered a gadget. Either way, it was a white elephant and for a year was a fit companion for my motorcycle, which was parked beside it in the barn. It was so awkward and cumbersome and required so many men to turn cranks and pull ropes that it stood idle. Only once, in my memory, was it used and that was to show a visiting veterinary student from Ames and me how it worked.

Metz Automobile

Uncle John had one of the first automobiles in Armstrong. It was called a Metz. I do not remember it except that it was pointed out to me in a junk pile behind a garage in Swea City. The wheels seemed no bigger than bicycle wheels and the body was of proportionate strength and weight. He told me how it had been shipped in a crate from Grand Rapids, Michigan with directions attached and how, on a couple of occasions, he had shoved it in from the country by hand with it had stalled or broken down.

Aeroplane

Uncle John was in the middle of a deal with a firm in Germany for an "aero-plane" when World War I cut the transaction off. He still talked about a plane and had what he knew was a far-fetched idea of a pair of rails extending out and upward from the upstairs of the barn to help boost the machine into the sky. It was far-fetched, of course, but at that time the description of a helicopter would have been equally fantastic. This was when authorities on aviation maintained that the extreme load limit of any plane would be, for all time, a pilot and one passenger.

John's Veterinary Practice

With a limited amount of schooling in his youth, with the English language still a problem, and the ever-present situation of being short of money, Uncle John showed great determination and tireless effort in completing the course of study at the Toronto Veterinary College. My mother has told of his leaving their place in South Dakota, driving a horse which was a graduation present from my father and mother, on a three-hundred-mile trip to Iowa where he was destined to become an outstanding veterinary practitioner and an individual of importance in his community. He continued his studies throughout the years and was, in every way, a well-educated man.

In his profession he was, as in other ways, far ahead of his time. Among his instruments were some of superior quality and special design that he had obtained directly from manufacturers in Germany and which, as yet, could not be furnished by the supply houses with which he normally dealt.

He corresponded with prominent veterinarians in Denmark and was the first veterinarian in the United States to use a method of treating parturient paresis that had been discovered by them. It was so successful that it was soon adopted as standard procedure everywhere.

He was especially interested in bacteriology and immunology. At a time when fistulous withers was a common ailment of horses, he often sent samples of purulent material to various laboratories in the hope it could be cultured and an immunizing agent, or one that could build up resistance to the infection, might be developed. From observation he learned that a high percentage of these afflicted horses came from farms where bovine contagious abortion was known to exist. He theorized on the probability of a cross-infection and said that when the causative agent was found both diseases would be under control. Many years later when the name of contagious abortion was changed to brucellosis, it was also found that the Brucella abortus was primarily responsible for fistulous withers. By the use of tests, vaccines, and sanitary measures brucellosis in cattle has been eradicated from the United States. The disease in horses has been self-eliminating with the almost total absence of horses on the farms.

The discovery that simultaneous injections of live hog cholera virus and anti-hog cholera serum into swine would produce an immunity to the disease was a great scientific breakthrough. It was also responsible for the most costly disease control program ever imposed upon the livestock industry.

Uncle John vaccinated his share of pigs and, I am sure, did not object to the fact that this enlarged his practice and increased his income. However, he realized that the continual use of live virus was perpetuating the disease rather than controlling it and assumed— along with many others—that this method would be abandoned as soon as sanity and sanitation combined to completely eradicate the disease. In the mid-teens he predicted this would occur within ten years, at the most. Instead it took a half a century before disease control authorities were able to bar the manufacture and use of live hog cholera virus and to institute effective measures which by now have made the United States free of hog cholera. The cost of the vaccination program can in no way be estimated, but it must have run into a figure of many billions of dollars.

In view of present-day knowledge, it may seem the theories, efforts, and accomplishments of the veterinarians of Uncle John's age group were not of very much importance. But when it is remembered that their steps, searching and often faltering, marked the path for the giant steps of later years, it will be realized they were important indeed.

Model T Ford

Most of my memories of the time spent in Armstrong, and of the following years as well, have much to do with automobiles. This is not surprising since automobiles were new, had been accepted as a dependable means of transportation, and transportation was so important to us in our work. I feel a listing of some of the things pertaining to motoring at that time—and which we took for granted as are the refinements of today taken for granted—might be interesting.

In Armstrong 1916 – Fred Sr. is at the wheel and John Thomsen is waving from the barn.

Of the approximately four hundred makes of automobiles manufactured in the United States during the first quarter of this century, probably a fourth were used and recognized in the Midwest. Of these, the Model T Fords were, by far, the most numerous and the make with which I was the best acquainted. The more expensive cars had refinements and improvements that were not built into the Fords for many years, one of which was the self-starter.

In the cold winters of northern Iowa and Minnesota, starting a Model T Ford was usually difficult and many strange methods were developed. One of the most common was to drain the oil from the crank case when the car was put away. It would be heated on the stove and poured back at the next starting time. Then with the front wheels blocked, the transmission set in high hear, one rear wheel jacked up to serve as a flywheel and the intake manifold heated with hot water or a torch, the operator began to spin the crank. It was often said that a strong back and a weak mind were the best of assets.

The headlights burned gas until about 1915 when the change to electric lights was made. The current was from the magneto and they were very poor.

The gas tank was under the front seat and the fuel was fed to the carburetor by gravity. Occasionally, when the tank was down to the bottom third or so and a hill was unusually steep, it would be necessary to turn around and drive up the grade in reverse.

Tires were expensive and were punctured and bruised easily. They blew out upon the slightest provocation. The front tires were kept at 60 pound pressure and the rear ones at 70 and were pumped up by hand. A highway was said to lead from Winnipeg to New Orleans as early as 1916. It was marked with a blue stenciled JH on poles, bridges and buildings. With few markings, road maps were not yet in existence. Unimproved dirt roads were common in Iowa and Missouri, and in the latter the pavement of one lane was poured one slab at a time with the second lane sometimes coming a couple of years later.

It was considered common courtesy to stop and offer to help another motorist in trouble. A sort of a bond existed between travelers, and in the evenings at the cabin camps the conversations often ended with talk of the day when it would be possible to drive from coast to coast without chains, shovel, or tow-rope.

The cabin camps were described fully by that name. As a rule the units were very cheaply built, with the studs and rafters exposed, and the furnishing very plain and often appearing to have been salvaged from the city dump. When new, they did have the pleasing smell of freshly sawed lumber, though.

It does not seem possible that the motorists of a half a century from now will consider our cars, highways, and traveling facilities as crude in comparison to those of fifty and sixty years ago.

Fred and Nina as Newlyweds

Upon graduating from the Kansas City Veterinary College in the spring of 1917, Nina and I rented a house in Farmington, Minnesota, bought a Model T Ford, and announced I was ready for business. The state board examinations were not to be given for several weeks but that was no worry since the board accepted this procedure and, as a rule, did not interfere with the activities of applicants during this interim, unless a complaint was made. After a few weeks, an older veterinarian in Farmington did object and, as a result, I was temporarily out of business.

For want of something better to do, we decided to drive the Ford back to Kansas City. In those days this was a trip not to be taken lightly so we first went to St. Paul to spend the night and to tell my folks of our plans. We arose for an early start the next morning and found that our car had been stolen. It seemed as if the finger of fate was getting kind of pushy.

I shall not burden you with events of the next couple of hectic days except to tell that the Ford was found near Elk River, Minnesota, the sheriff had it taken to a garage, I went up and paid the ransom, and we started south with the first stop at Armstrong. Since we had ample time, we borrowed a tent from Harry Helgesen and camped for a few days in someone's pasture on Silver Lake up near the Minnesota line. It was a pleasant interlude before continuing on our way.

With few marked roads and no road maps, we threaded through Algona, Fort Dodge, Atlantic, and Villisca in Iowa and on to St.

Joseph and Kansas City. In spite of having been gone nearly two months, no one seemed to have changed very much. The return trip was easier and we arrived at Armstrong with little trouble but pretty well flat broke.

Uncle John remarked that he was thinking of trading in his year-old Ford for a new one and if I was interested, he would trade with me and give me a hundred and fifty dollars to boot. It did not take long for me to accept. So after a day or two we headed for St. Paul and the session with the examining board.

In the cool of the morning the car ran as smoothly as a well-oiled sewing machine and the feeling of the wad of bills in my hip pocket was softer than a cushion of silk. It was a beautiful morning. We crossed into Minnesota and on the smooth gravel roads, with the top down and the wind whistling past the windshield, we fairy flew. It was a beautiful day.

As the day drew on, the sun became hotter and the gravel road began taking its toll of our tires. Three blew out before reaching St. Paul and the fourth a few days later. It was a real good car, though, and sold well when I left to report for military duty a few weeks later.

Incidentally, the secretary of the examining board called on the phone at five o'clock in the morning the day after the examinations to tell me I had passed. He suggested I go out and "Kill the Irishman."[21]

---

[21] I think Fred took that to mean that he should go out and celebrate with more liquor than would kill an Irishman. RJT

John Thomsen with his son, John G. Thomsen – about 1922

Last Visit to Armstrong

The next time we were in Armstrong was in the summer of 1920. Nina, Fred, and I had been in Kansas City and, by pre-arrangement, came home that way to pick up my father and mother who were visiting there. The highlight of the occasion was a family picnic. The group included our cousin John— Sabina's uncle—and his wife Fannie. I believe they were living at Fairmont at the time.

That was our last visit with Uncle John.

* * * *

When you were about two years old, Nina, Fred [Jr.], and I spent a night with your mother and you on our way to, as usual, Kansas City. When we arrived, you were playing in a small tent in the yard at about the same place Uncle John had his ever-bearing strawberry plants.

I do not know if it was your birthday, but for some reason I felt an urge to get you a present and went to the hardware store and bought a pocket knife. Your mother, with much better judgment than mine, promptly impounded it until you were bigger. I hope you got it back in due time because it was a good knife.

That was our last trip to Armstrong.

* * * *

It has been fun, John, to write this rambling recital of related recollections. I hope you will find something in it to help fill out your picture of life in Armstrong nearly sixty years ago.

There is not much I can add except to say that your father was quite a man in every sense of the word, and your mother belonged in a class of equal distinction. It was my good fortune to live with them as I did and to know them so well.

So, I shall close with a quotation from an anonymous quipster which I am sure Uncle John would have enjoyed. "If I have said anything I am sorry for, I am damn glad of it."

Sincerely Yours,

Fred Hansen

Independence, Missouri, January 14, 1974

Then Fred responded to a letter from John.

January 25, 1974

Dear John and Pearle:

I am glad you found the stories about Armstrong so interesting. Your complimentary response pleased me greatly although I know they could not have been quite that good. It did take a little more than a few days to complete it though. In fact, I piddled away at it, an hour now and an hour then, over a period of weeks. The incidents I told of were so deeply etched in my mind that remembering was no problem. My difficulty was to keep them down to a reasonable length without losing the gist of the stories. This applies to the present paragraph which could be condensed by half. Anyway it was fun.

Not being the best typist, I did not try to make carbon copies but, instead, resorted to a Xerox copier when I was through. About a third of the way through, the machine spluttered and belched out a cloud of smoke in place of the copied sheet. I wondered if it was rejecting something I had said but learned that it did his every so often without reason.

We too have enjoyed the meetings and visits with you and your family over the years and hope they can keep on for a long time to come.

We hope you will have plenty of snow for your ski trip to Colorado. Our eighteen inches has melted and no more is needed here.

Sincerely, Fred

Chapter 4

Nina's Childhood Story, by Nina Strahan Hansen

Here Nina tells of her childhood from 1897 to 1917, leading from Indian Territory, Oklahoma, through several moves in Oklahoma, Kansas, and Missouri and ending with events leading to meeting Fred Jr. Nina's stories from Oklahoma evoke visions of Laura Ingalls Wilder's descriptions in her semi-autobiographical Little House on the Prairie *series. Though Wilder's experience happened some thirty years earlier, we can assume many similarities. The Ingalls family life on the Oklahoma prairie (Little House on the Prairie) happened from 1869 to 1871, and the time in a dugout house in Minnesota* (On the Banks of Plum Creek) *was in 1874.*

This is the Summer of 1977. I have been asked by my family to write about my childhood.

Birth in Perry, Oklahoma, Indian Territory

On the 15th of May, 1897 Nina Pearl Strahan was born in Perry, Oklahoma, Indian Territory. I was the fourth child of Hendricks Pinkney Strahan and Mary Anna Strahan. My childhood was a normal, ordinary one.

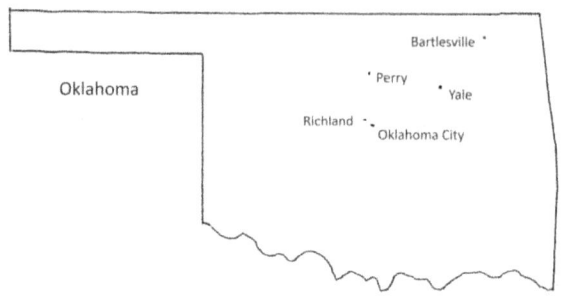

Map of Oklahoma

Yale, Oklahoma

There was one episode that stands out in my memory. I was 5 or 6 years old at the time. My father and his brother, uncle Bill, decided to go to Yale, Oklahoma, where a railroad was being built and there was plenty of work to be had. My Uncle Bill was a gambler and I am sure he didn't intend to do any hard labor.

The trip from Perry to Yale was made by two covered wagons and four horses. When we got there, in a couple of days, the only place that was vacant was an old dugout or cave. After cleaning it out and rebuilding the old broken-down steps, we moved in. It was a terrible place for my mother and her five children. My youngest sister, Anna, three years old, became lost one day and the searching party found her down by the river, stuck in the mud. [Missing word(s)?] We spent Xmas in this cave. Lynne, my oldest sister, and I can remember how happy we were to find a little doll, an orange, and some nuts in our stockings on Xmas morning. In the Spring my Grandmother Strahan sent my father money to come back to Perry and we went by train.

Perry, Oklahoma

My father got a job working for a Mr. Reeves in his secondhand furniture store. Dad repaired old furniture. When the road shows or a circus came, they would put their handbills and advertisements in the windows of the store and give free passes to Mr. Reeves. He always gave them to my father. Dad would take us kids to see the plays in the old Opera House and the circuses in a pasture on the outskirts of Perry. When my grandmother died in 1903 we moved into their house which seemed like a mansion. There were two bedrooms upstairs, one for us girls and one for my brothers, Oak and Park.

Grandpa Strahan was very active in the Grand Army of the Republic. He also was active in civic and political affairs. He was married in 1904 to Mrs. Emma Pomeroy and moved to her house. He gave us a little money once in a while, and Mama would allow Lynne and me to walk around the Square and buy a nickel dish of ice cream or a sack of popcorn. There was always a lot of action around the square, Indians and cowboys. The big Court House was in the center of the Square—hitching rails for the horses and a lawn with benches for people to sit on. The Indians would sit on the ground with blankets around them—mostly Cherokee Indians. They were good Indians.

On the outside of the Square were shops and stores. Some of the old buildings are still there with a new face lift. The old Opera House was a gay place in its day. With a saloon nearby, some of the patrons got pretty rough. My Uncle Bill threatened to shoot the villain in one play for spitting in the girl's face. His comrades had to grab him and take his gun away. It was the talk of the town.

Visits to Grandma and Grandpa Dillon in Richland, OK

Riding the train to Richland, Oklahoma, to visit my Grandma and Grandpa Dillon, was a big thrill. It was probably 75 or 80 miles but it took several hours to get there. We always had a lunch along to eat on the train.

My Grandma lived on a small farm. There were a few cattle, always a little calf in the barn to pet, a few pigs, and chickens.

Grandma would let me help her churn butter. It took a lot of churning to make butter. It was the old plunger type churn—maybe there wasn't any other kind—but Grandma and I would take turns at it until she could tell when the butter was ready to dish up. Then she would work it with a paddle and rinse it with cold water and a big lump of butter would be ready for the crocks which she would carry to the storm cave to harden. Everyone had a storm cave or cellar where they kept food and milk and also used it if a bad storm approached.

The railroad track and a ravine ran between Grandma's farm and Aunt Nellie's. This ravine had a little water in it, especially after a rain. On either side there were trees and wild grape vines hanging from them. Our cousins and us kids would hang on the vines and swing across the ravine. Sometimes they would break and we would fall in the water. It was only a foot deep if we were lucky to have any at all. It was great fun and a lot different than living in Perry. We made this trip to Richland several times while we were living in Perry. Richland was a very small town with a church, school, general store, blacksmith shop, and a few little houses. Now they are all gone, the railroad is no more, and the ravine is just a little ditch. At least some of us still have our pleasant memories.

Oklahoma Statehood

In 1907 Oklahoma became the 46th State of the Union. I was ten years old. Perry was a wild and rowdy town for several days. There were celebrations every day with fireworks, cowhands, ranchers, and Indians. My Dad would not let us girls go around the Square but some of the celebrating spilled over in our street. We lived a block from the Square and could hear the guns and fireworks and people yelling and shouting. Dad said there were fights and a lot of drunks all over town.

We liked Grandpa's house. There were peach trees and a grape arbor from the kitchen porch to the barn yard gate, where Grandpa kept a horse and buggy. I remember the grape jelly and peach cobblers Mama made. We surely lived good those days. The Methodist church where we went to Sunday School gave us a fancy little card with a picture of Jesus and a lamb, and every Sunday the teacher would put a silver star on it, then on special days we would get a little gold star. I wonder whatever became of my card.

Bartlesville, Oklahoma—Pinky

A lot of things were left behind when we made the move to Bartlesville, Oklahoma. My father, Oak, and Park got jobs at the smelter plant, and Dad rented a little four room house and sent for Mama and us four girls, Lynne, Anna, Eveline, and me.

After we had been there several months, Mama had a little baby boy. We called him Pinky. He was named for my Dad, Hendricks Pinkney. He died at the age of seven months. It was a very sad time for our family and I was old enough to understand why my father had cried at his mother's funeral. At that time I sat beside him and cried because he was crying. I was six years old. Now I was crying because we had lost a darling little baby brother whom we all loved. The neighbor ladies came and helped my mother clean the house and cooked some meals. Pinky was put in a little white coffin and a preacher came to the house for the services. We all walked to the cemetery. The men carried the casket and we followed along. The cemetery was only five or six blocks from our house. For several days Lynne and I would pick some wild flowers and put them on Pinky's grave. My folks joined the Church of God shortly after that sadness and were baptized.

Carnival

One day Mama let us go to the carnival that was in town. We had a couple of nickels and the first thing we did was to ride the merry-go-round. I got on a horse, hanging on, but when I handed the man my nickel I went flying through the air. The next thing I knew I was in a tent and a very beautiful lady was washing my face. I had landed on my head. (Now it can be told why I am so dumb.) The lady was dressed in fancy, sparkling clothes and all painted up. She said she was a snake charmer with the show. A man took us home in a horse and buggy. Mama told him I was a tomboy. She was glad I wasn't hurt too much.

Wichita, Kansas

When we left Bartlesville to go to Wichita, Kansas I hated to leave my best girlfriend, an Indian girl Bessie Tinker, and my first boyfriend, Raymond Darling. Dad, Oak, and Park went to Wichita and found work. Later Dad sent for Mama and us girls. Mama sold all the old furniture, packed the trunks and valises, and we arrived in Wichita, ready to settle down again. Dad had rented a house and bought furniture so it didn't take long. Oh, those movin' Strahans!!

Our stay in Wichita was not long but a few things happened. I became a teenager. Mama had a baby boy named Joseph. Dad said he took the place of little Pinky. We were crazy about him. Lynne was a young lady and got a job with the National Biscuit Company. I was eager to grow up so I could work, too. I didn't realize how quickly it would happen. Park joined the Navy. Then it happened again. Dad and Oak went to Oklahoma City, found work, and sent for us.

Oklahoma City

We finally got settled in "Packing Town." The men worked for the Wilson Packing Company, Lynne worked, and the rest of us went to school. Mama wasn't in good health. Dad told Lynne and me she had a tumor, to help her and be good girls. I helped with the washing and kneaded the bread twice a week. We would bake eight big loaves at a time. Then one day the big tumor was gone and we had a baby sister, Genevieve (Jenny for short). All is well that ends— Well.

Dad played the "mouth organ" pretty well. We would sit on the front porch, he would play, and we would sing the old tunes like My Old Kentucky Home, Swanee River, Old Black Joe, and Home Sweet Home were our favorites. He also played "The Irish Washer Woman" and "The Arkansas Traveler" while we would clap our hands. Then he would finish by imitating a locomotive engine. First he would go with a slow "chug-chug", pick up steam and really make it roll, ending with a shrill whistle. I guess the neighbors liked it. We never heard a complaint from any of them.

Mama was easygoing and a sweet person. She was married and had a baby when she was fifteen years old. In spite of all her hard work and having babies, she lived to be ninety-two years old. The last twenty years of her life she had it easy visiting with her children. Her permanent home was with Anna and Soren. Dad died at the age of eighty.

We had a lot of fun growing up in Oklahoma City. I took training to become a telephone operator but [when] I was assigned a job to work at night my father wouldn't let me take it. I worked for a short while in the bacon packing department at the packing house. I had a couple of boyfriends. The one I liked best was George Leach, whose father was a Kansas wheat farmer. Lynne was married to Roy English. Oak and I stood up for her.

Dad had an accident at the job and received a settlement. He worked in the lard refinery department. One day he was using a steam hose on a lard vat, standing on a cat-walk six feet high. The steam hose had too much pressure and went out of control, knocking him to the floor. He got a broken wrist and was scalded. After he was healed and back to normal, he received the settlement. With this money he and Oak went to Kansas City, Missouri. The same old story but with a good ending. Mama and the family came to a new place and we got settled again, this time at 1300 Cleveland Avenue.

Before we left Oklahoma City, I became a drop-out, worked, and bought my own clothes. One outfit was a hobble skirt, split up the

118

back with a green taffeta underskirt that showed when I walked. It was very up-to-date. I took Little Joe with me to our first baseball game. We rode the street car. With my hobble skirt and Joe by my side, I felt really grown up. He always was my favorite brother.

Kansas City, Missouri

I did not feel too badly about coming to Kansas City. I got a job at Montgomery Wards. My wage was $8.00 a week. I gave Mama $4.00 for room and board. There was an accident one day at work. A large group of us girls dashed for the freight elevator on the eighth floor when the five-minute bell went off at the end of our lunch hour. The operator started and realized he had overloaded the elevator. He couldn't stop it and we went down in a hurry, crashing in the pit. The steel door had to be pried open to let us out. Everyone was screaming but there were no serious injuries. I got a two weeks paid vacation for having two sore knees and a lame back. It paid off by being packed in like sardines; we just fell on each other.

Fred

By this time I was eighteen years old and I didn't have a boyfriend. A girl next door, Cora Wheeler, asked me if I would double date. Her boyfriend was a student at the Kansas City Veterinary College. He had a friend who wanted to meet a girl. So that is how it all happened. Fred came into my life. He was also a student at the Veterinary College. He came out often and we would walk over to the Mozart silent movie theater on 12th Street. Once in awhile, we would ride the streetcar downtown to a play. We also walked to Grove Park on Benton Boulevard to watch the crowd. Then there were evenings when we sat on the front porch and Dad would get a pail of beer. "Onion sandwiches" were a special treat with a small glass of beer. Fred's roommate, Phil Radford, would taunt him about being with the "Onion King's" daughter.

When the Spring semester was over, in 1916, Fred went to Armstrong, Iowa, to work with his Uncle John, a veterinarian, until he returned for the Fall term at the K.C.V.C. By this time, we knew we were in love. We became engaged and he gave me a lovely diamond ring. I was pretty proud to show the ring to my girlfriends at "Monkey Wards." Fred attended college and I worked, with dates on weekends mostly. Of course we talked a lot about getting married.

Then one evening after seeing a movie at the Mozart, where the young couple eloped, Fred dared me to meet him the next day at 12th and Main at a certain time and we would elope. I guess he didn't have to pull my leg. I met him, he had bought a wedding ring. We got on the Interurban that took us to Liberty, Missouri, went to the Court House, got a license, and were married by a Justice of the Peace. This was the 3rd day of March, 1917. I have never regretted that day.

This ends my so-called "Childhood Story." I am pleased my family urged me to write it. Many memories came back that have been locked up inside. Whether it has been worthwhile or interesting, it has given me the satisfaction of knowing I could do it.

There is a big gap between 1917 and 1977, covering our life together, which has been a good, fulfilling span, and I hope perhaps Fred and I can fill that gap together. We have a lot of good things to tell and a wonderful family to write about. May we be granted the time to do this.

So ends my story.

Independence, Missouri

September 10, 1977 Nina Strahan Hansen

Chapter 5

Sixty Years . . . and More, Part One,

by Frederic W. Hansen, Sr.

When Fred or Nina refer to "Mother" it is to Fred's mother, Sophia Hansen. When they use "Mom" or "Dad," they are referring to each other.

Recently we have both written about the things we remember from our childhood and teenage days. Those days ended with the trip to Liberty on March 3rd, 1917 and our marriage by a Justice of the Peace, which Nina told about. Now we shall try to combine our efforts and tell some of the happenings of the following years. To begin with, 1917 was an eventful year.

Newlyweds and Graduation, Farmington, Minnesota

Following our marriage, which probably surprised us as much as it did others, we rented a small furnished apartment for the remaining weeks of my school year. Few would describe it as a "Honeymoon Cottage" but to us it was something special. While Nina kept house I attended classes, anxiously awaited the day of graduation when the future would really open. During this time, war was declared against Germany and, with many of my classmates, I applied for service in the Veterinary Corps of the U.S. Army. A commission as a 2nd Lieutenant came a few days later.

The date of graduation finally arrived. During the day we had our luggage taken to the Union Depot and bought tickets to Farmington, Minnesota, where we intended to locate. In the evening, when the oratory was over, the diplomas presented, and the deposit on the cap and gown had been refunded, we took the street car to the depot and boarded the train. As we sped through the night, we felt sure that Opportunity had knocked and that prosperity and success were just ahead. At that time we did not know—and to this day have not learned—how to tell the difference between the knocking of Opportunity and the idle drumming of the fingers of Fate.

After finding a place to live in Farmington, renting an empty barn, and buying a factory fresh Model T Ford (delivered price $373.00), we were in business. The fact that I had no license did not seem important since it was the custom to allow new applicants to practice until the State Board examinations were given in June. With getting settled, visits with my folks in St. Paul, and a few calls coming in, we managed to appear busy. About that time, it was found that Nina was pregnant. We knew this was a situation that often-confronted grownups and one that did not require immediate attention. Our life in Farmington was going fine. Then the unexpected happened.

Contrary to custom, my competitor complained about my lack of a license. His brother-in-law was the County Attorney. The members of the Examining Board, whom I contacted, were sympathetic but powerless to interfere. It seemed the best thing for us to do would be to take a vacation. We decided to drive to Kansas City but before leaving went to St. Paul to spend the night with my folks and tell them of our plans. During the night our car was stolen. The police offered little hope of finding it but it was found in a ditch at Elk River. After redeeming it from the garage to which the sheriff had taken it, we began our trip.

At Armstrong, Iowa, we spent a few days with my Uncle John

and his wife, Kirstine. Then over unmarked and poorly kept roads we worked our way south to Kansas City. We stayed a week or ten days and then returned to St. Paul in time for the two-day State Board Examinations. At six o'clock the following morning the secretary, Dr. Hay, called to tell me I had passed and was duly licensed.

The reaction to the whole affair seemed to be in our favor and brought calls and recognition that would not have come otherwise. On the strength of this, we rented a larger house with all the rooms on one floor and better suited to a growing family. So we carried on from day to day while awaiting the next turn of events, which was not a surprise.

World War— U.S. Army in Battle Creek, Michigan

Early in September a telegram came directing me to report to Camp Custer, Battle Creek, Michigan, for active military duty. We packed and stored our belongings, sold the Ford, and took the train for Battle Creek. One incident of that train trip stands out clearly in my mind. Along in the middle of the night Nina's unpredictable appetite called for a bacon and tomato sandwich. The porter said he would go back to the diner and see what he could find, returning shortly with probably the biggest and juiciest sandwich every consumed in the small space of a Pullman berth.

At Camp Custer I was assigned to the Remount Depot along with a few other newly arrived Veterinary second lieutenants. The Remount Depot was an arrangement of corrals and stables with a capacity of over 12,000 horses and mules with frequent ingoing and outgoing shipments. With no guidelines, the commanding officer suggested we work out our own veterinary program. I quickly chose the task of patrolling the many acres of corrals, with a small group of riders, to move ailing animals to the hospital barns. This responsibility soon included the general supervision of the corrals, the judging of the condition of new arrivals and the determination of fitness of those shipped out. It was steady work but interesting and, in most ways, enjoyable.

Soon after our arrival at Battle Creek Nina found a room in a private home. With her ability to make friends, she had no trouble becoming acquainted. Two or three of my colleagues were accompanied by their wives also, so the group suppers at the Busy Bee Café were always pleasant affairs.

Fred Jr.

With the time for the arrival of the baby coming closer, Nina left for Kansas City in November. Fred Jr. was born on December 12th. Since I had arranged for a leave at Christmas time, he was well into his second week before I saw him. Frankly I was somewhat awed by him and by the fact that he was really ours and greatly impressed by the ease with which Nina handled and took care of him. I returned to Camp Custer, with Nina planning to follow when the baby was older and stronger.

1917 was, indeed, an eventful year.

On January 18th, 1918 it was ten degrees below zero in Kansas City. That was the day Mom and Fred, who was five weeks old, left for Battle Creek. The train was snowbound for forty-eight hours near a small town in Iowa. It was a welcome sight when the two finally arrived, two days late. She said that the cars had been warm and the diner served plenty of good food. There had been no shortage of volunteer babysitters either. There had been no real hardship but a lot of anxiety.

The routine at the camp went on as before. I was able to spend the nights in town except in cases of special duty. One event of importance was my promotion. I became a first Lieutenant. Some of our friends were transferred but replaced, so our immediate group of associates kept on an even balance.

In May of 1918 my brother, George, died suddenly. It was the first death in either of our immediate families in many years. I obtained a leave and we went to St. Paul for the funeral. This was the first time Father, Mother, or my sister, Olga, had seen the baby. We felt that the attention they gave him helped in some way to ease the shock and grief of George's death.

When we returned to Battle Creek, we found a place to stay with a family in a small village called Level Ark. It was only a mile or so from camp so I rode a horse forth and back. As usual Nina was soon acquainted with everyone. Another veterinary officer rented a house and brought his wife and children. It was a pleasant summer. The latter part of September, Nina and Fred went back to Kansas City for a visit. When they came back we found a place in town.

The next big event was Armistice Day—or rather Armistice Night—November 11th. The whole town went wild, with parades crossing, colliding, and joining each other until there wasn't a street without a full-blown parade. If a car ran out of gas, fifty people would push it along. In a borrowed Ford roadster, we were held in line for an hour or so before we could break away. For noise, lack of leadership, and enthusiasm it was a parade to remember.

With the war ended the Army began selling now surplus animals at public auction sales. This added to our work. Speculators bought and shipped them in carload lots.

At about the same time, my mother's letters became more gloomy, with thoughts of Christmas without George, so Nina took the baby to St. Paul, early in December, knowing this would brighten the Holidays somewhat. I had hoped to come for Christmas but with our push of activity I did not make it until after New Year. Everyone seemed happy with the memories of Fred's first birthday and first Christmas. He was ready at any time to demonstrate his ability to blow out candles or a match with, now and then, a shot at a light bulb. When it was time for us to leave, the folks suggested that we leave the baby with them for the few weeks until I could expect my discharge from the Army. So we went back alone. There were times when we were not sure we had done the best thing but it worked out fine.

Discharge from the Army—To Farmington, Minnesota

My discharge came on February 8th. I drew my current pay, collected the $60.00 severance pay which the Government benevolently bestowed upon each departing serviceman, raffled off my saddle for $100.00, bought a suit of civilian clothes, and we left for St. Paul. Mom kept thinking the train was behind schedule all the way and, I admit, I also thought it was not running at full speed. The family had all enjoyed the period of babysitting and Fred was now able to blow out two matches at a time with, as before, an occasional random shot at a light bulb.

The first step towards resuming practice was the purchase of another Model T Ford. We learned that a veterinarian had moved to Farmington shortly after we left and was by now well established. Without very much thought we decided to settle in Lakeville, only five miles away. It did not turn out well and by September I was glad to get a job as field veterinarian with the State Livestock Sanitary Board. At first we moved into an apartment but later bought a small house a mile or so from where my folks lived. During this time I was trying to find a suitable place to again begin a veterinary practice. A year or so later it appeared that Wadena was the place.

A middle-aged veterinarian there had become a drug addict and had been sentenced to a term in the penitentiary for breaking into a drug store and a physician's office in search for drugs. I spoke with the County agent, farmers, and businessmen there, including a younger veterinarian with whom I was acquainted, and most were of the opinion that he could not stand the "cure" and would not live to the end of his term. He surprised everyone by coming back in a year, hale, hearty, and cured. There was not enough business to support the three of us. It was decision time again when my father came up with what seemed a very good idea.

Pelican Rapids, Minnesota

Father had always been most interested in farming and livestock raising. Since his retirement he had speculated in real estate and a few years before had bought a 320 acre farm at Pelican Rapids. It was being operated by tenants. He suggested stocking it and turning it over to us in the belief that a farm and a veterinary practice would be an unbeatable combination. It sounded real good to us. In the Spring of 1923 we moved to the farm. Fred was five years old. This kind of life was, however, just as new to Mom as it was to him.

That first summer, Father and I puttered and patched with never a shortage of jobs to be done, while Nina became acquainted with the long hours and hard work of life on a farm as well as the feeling of isolation and loneliness, where close neighbors were a mile or so away, and Fred found he had almost a whole world of his own to explore. This was the start of ten years of hills and valleys, hopes and disappointment and enough experiences to fill volumes in the telling. Most of these must, of course, be left out, although a few were unusual enough and, hopefully interesting enough to be included here. Such a one occurred on a hot August afternoon of that first summer.

Lightning Storm

I had planned to go to town for a load of cement, but instead of taking the truck decided to use a wagon with a team of horses that were becoming somewhat unruly because of lack of work and exercise. With an umbrella, in case of a shower, Mom and Fred climbed on the seat and we started out. The horses were restive and looking for something that might frighten them. Storm clouds began gathering in the west and by the time we left town the sky was dark and the thunder and lightning much closer. The storm broke with a sudden fury just as we were starting down a long hill. As Nina tried to open the umbrella the horses saw it over their blinders and had the excuse for running that they had been waiting for.

For the next minute, which seemed like an hour, I was the most helpless I have ever been. The horses were at a full gallop with the heavy load pushing them on down the hill and the lines were so wet and slippery that I could not grip them to gain any control. As the road leveled off at the foot of the hill, I was able to turn them onto a stubble field where the weight of the load on the soft ground slowed them down quickly. They stopped beside a load of bundles where a farmer, named Mr. Moses, was waiting out the storm in the shelter of his wide load. He invited us to join him but we were already wet and so thanked him and drove on. A couple of minutes later a blinding flash of lightning and a sharp clap of thunder seemed to engulf us. It was so startling the horses stopped, as if stunned momentarily and then went on. That bolt of lightning was too close for comfort. We arrived home to learn the word had come over the telephone an hour earlier that Mr. Moses' load of bundles had been struck by lightning, killing him and his horses instantly.

Farming and Veterinary Practice

In the late Summer and through Fall we took in most of the farm sales in the neighborhood, buying livestock and equipment. At the same time a building crew was remodeling the inside of the barn and erecting a silo. By the time of the first heavy snow, we were settled for the Winter. The car was put away and all travel, whether to visit neighbors, make veterinary calls, or trips to town was by horses and sleds. We did have a daily mail delivery, a party telephone line, and the first radio in the community. It was a long winter but the monotony was broken by a visit by Nina's father, mother, and teenage brother and sister, Joe and Jennie. The youngsters enjoyed the novelty of the cold, the huge snow drifts, and the almost daily sleigh rides. After three or four weeks they all left with later visits being made in the Summer.

With the Spring planting done, the fields turned green with the promise of a good crop, our cattle herd was gradually increasing, and things looked bright. Then in June a cyclone or tornado completely demolished the barn and silo and badly damaged another silo that had not yet been put up. Such storms were so rare at that time that few people carried insurance against them. The loss set us back about as far as we could go. We managed, however, a long-term loan from a State-owned agency that had been recently established, rebuilt the barn and silos, and awaited whatever might come next.

The next few years were better. Our livestock improved, crops were good, and prices were quite high. A general boom was sweeping the country, work was plentiful, and wages in the cities were said to be $5.00 a day. At times this made it difficult to keep hired help. Although we seldom had trouble in this regard it did happen once in a while. One instance was at harvest time. For a few days, Mom, who a short time before had not even driven a horse, would hurry through her chores, come to the field and drive the five horses on the binder while Fred and I would try to catch up with putting the bundles in shocks. But all in all, it was a good period with a lot of hope for the future.

Gradual changes were taking place in our lives too. We had become established as part of the community. Fred attended school a mile and a half away over open prairie, often riding his pony, Rex. At times, we boarded the teacher. Mom was elected treasurer of the school board, an office she continued to hold even after we left the farm. In the summers, Jeanette, Olga's adopted daughter, spent her vacations with us, and many of the folks from Kansas City came to visit.

About this time Nina became interested in 4H work and started the first club in that part of the county. Later she organized two more in adjoining townships and worked with the Extension Service as an adviser for other clubs. The first one, the Scrambler 4H club, is the one best remembered. For his project Fred had a roan Shorthorn calf named Pete. We all helped with his care and in so doing made him into a regular pet. By the time of the County Fair, he seemed to know just how to show off his 900 pounds to the best advantage. He did not win the first prize but came in fifth in competition with 90 others, which was not bad since winners and losers all shared the same destiny. Arrangements were made to ship them all to market. When his Mom and I came in the show barn the next day, he acted as if he was glad to see us. We folded his blanket, replaced his shiny halter with a rope, picked up buckets and brushes, gave him a goodbye pat on the rump, and left. For many miles we did not look at each other or speak for fear of bursting into tears. The next year's calf was named Mike. We learned to treat him as a calf and not as a family pet.

Four Generations in 1943: Fred Jr., Sharon, Sophia, Fred Sr.

After the years of prosperity, the Great Depression began. Prices were so low they did not keep up the expenses of the farm. To help with this I began working on "Area Tests," which I shall try to explain. The Federal Government, working with the many states, had started a program to eradicate Bovine Tuberculosis by testing all the cattle in the country and destroying the diseased animals. It was accomplished by taking a county at a time and employing enough veterinarians to complete the test in two weeks. Most of the veterinarians I knew welcomed a chance at the work whenever it was offered during the moneyless days of the Depression.

Four Generations in 1943: Florence Hansen, Sharon, Sophia, Kirstine Thomsen, Nina Hansen – 1943.

Move to Town

With Fred's first year in high school we decided to leave the farm chores to hired help and so rented an apartment in town. This worked out real well in many ways. My father died in February of 1932 after a month's illness. During this time and after his death, Nina spent a great deal of time with my mother, which she could not have done had we been on the farm. It also made it possible for me to make the many trips to Saint Paul, which seemed so necessary at the time.

As if the Depression alone was not enough to contend with it was accompanied by a drouth which increased in severity each year. It reached from Oklahoma and Colorado into a large section of western Minnesota, creating the huge Dust Bowl of the Thirties. By the summer of 1933 it was plain there would be no crop on the farm worth harvesting. About the middle of August we sold the livestock, machinery, and equipment at an auction sale and bade farewell to

"Hansen's Folly" with mixed emotions, including sighs of relief.

This has probably sounded like a tale of woe but it actually was not that bad. We had our health, a veterinary practice that was providing a comfortable living, and had salvaged something out of the Depression by holding the sale when we did and not a year later. Then, too, there were other pleasant things to remember, including good neighbors, neighborhood parties, picnics and outings at the lakes, the fairs and 4H meetings, and so many more.

During those years we made almost yearly trips to Kansas City and enjoyed the times the relatives came to visit us for their vacations and days of fishing. We drove to St. Paul quite often and were pleased when Father, Mother, and Olga came to see us. Father, of course, came most often and was never happier than when he could shed his dress-up clothes and pitch into the work as if everything depended upon it.

In summing up the ten years on the farm, we agree that there were more pluses than minuses.

Four Generations in 1943: Sharon, Fred Jr., Sophia, Fred Sr.

Work for Cattle-buying Program

In 1934 the drouth reached its peak. Huge clouds of dust,

132

beginning hundreds of miles away, blackened the skies and carried ton after ton of powdered topsoil from the plains to the eastern part of the country. By July the pastures and fields were so bare the Government started a cattle-buying program in several western Minnesota counties. Practicing veterinarians were employed to carry out the work. I was assigned to the two adjoining counties to the west, Wilkin and Clay, and spent the next two months appraising, signing vouchers for, and supervising the shipment of literally thousands of head of cattle. Then in the Fall it began to rain and the fields were soon green again. The drouth had ended and the dust bowl would soon be history. In a couple of years streams were running, lakes were filling up, and crops were good. Most important of all, prosperity had returned.

The area tests for tuberculosis were completed in the last counties in the State in the Summer of 1934. They would be retested and retested time and again for years to come, but the results of the work in the earlier counties had been so good the program was considered a great success in the 10 or 12 years it had been in operation. The percentage of tuberculosis in cattle had been reduced to a minimum but, better yet, the county and state sanitariums were cutting down their facilities in expectation of closing in a few years because of a lack of patients. It was gratifying to those of us who had worked on these tests to realize how much had been accomplished.

The depression tapered off as the drouth ended. The "Bank Holidays" were over. With the Government's assurance that deposits were now safe, people became more free with the spending of their money. Business in general was good, as if trying to make up for the preceding few years.

New Home in Pelican Rapids

Across the street from our apartment, in the Ebersville Building, was a vacant lot that had been the location of the Post Office years before. It was for sale. We bought it and then began visualizing a Cape Cod style brick house with dormer windows and a fireplace. Nina first drew a floor plan with details being added and corrections being made until it was turned over to an architect who translated it into a blueprint for use by the builders. From then on there was nothing to do but build. So in the Fall of 1935 we moved into our house. Although some alterations have been made, it still stands as square and true as it was when the neighbors gave us a housewarming party over forty years ago.

The mid-thirties were busy years. Practice was exceedingly good but with long days and endless miles of driving. Mom was as busy as I with her work and that of the office. One important part was relaying calls and messages to me in the country, over rural telephone lines, in the days before car telephones and citizen's band radios. We managed, however, to take part in the activities of organizations such as the American Legion, the Commercial Club, the Lake Region Veterinary Society, and the Minnesota Veterinary Medical Association.

Nina Hansen with Sharon and Claudia.

In the American Legion we held related offices of Post Commander of Victor Cornell Post Number 17 and that of the

President of the Auxiliary at the same time. The Post was active in many local projects but the highlights during our terms were the district convention at Fergus Falls and the State convention at Albert Lea. The Pelican Rapids Commercial Club had no auxiliary. In fact, the membership was limited to men. It was extremely civic-minded but did occasionally display a lighter side. One of these times was during my year of office when several of us rehearsed a home talent play to put on at farmer's clubs and other small towns in the area. After one or two performances it became a game between us of ad-libbing and creation of impromptu scenes and situations so that the author would not have recognized his effort nor claimed it if he had. It was a lot of fun and served well as a business booster.

The Lake Region Veterinary Society was composed of 30 or 35 practitioners who tried to meet a few times each year—usually at a lake or picnic ground—to visit and discuss mutual problems. It had no auxiliary either, but the wives who prepared the picnic baskets had much to do with its success. It gradually faded away as have most of its members. While it lasted it was an example of friendship and congeniality. As time went on Mom and I again teamed up as president of the organization and president of the auxiliary in the offices of the Minnesota Veterinary Medical Association. For a man and wife to hold such positions twice seems quite unusual.

Life in Pelican Rapids soon fell into a sort of routine pattern with, of course, some changes from time to time. Fred graduated from high school, attended the North Dakota State College at Fargo for his pre-med course, and in the Fall of 1936 entered the Veterinary College of the University of Kansas at Manhattan. We made our customary trips to visit the family at Kansas City. (For some years the folks had lived in Independence, only a few miles from their former address. The latter location will be used from here on.)

Fred Hansen Sr. with Sharon and Claudia.

Minnesota State Livestock Sanitary Board

On these trips we usually went to both Independence, Missouri, and Manhattan, Kansas. On one occasion Nina's father and mother came back with us for a stay of a few weeks. They had not been in Minnesota since before we left the farm and so had not seen our house or the change in the way we lived. We took them home after a good visit. With our way of life, seemingly, so well established it was a surprise to receive an offer from the State Livestock Sanitary Board of an appointment as a field veterinarian.

The offer was inviting. I had always had a liking for disease control work, the salary was good, the work would not be as strenuous as in practice, and we could continue making our home in Pelican Rapids. There would be a great deal of traveling but with cars and roads so much improved, that was no problem. With few household responsibilities, Mom could come along whenever she chose. So for the next four years we traveled up and down and forth and back on every highway in Minnesota, staying mostly at County Seat hotels but with frequent trips to St. Paul and enough time at home to keep in contact with our friends there. The work was varied enough to be continually interesting. It ran from investigations and assignments of short duration to supervising area tests for tuberculosis and brucellosis that lasted for two or three weeks. Our first vacation was the first paid vacation I had had since my employment by the Sanitary Board nearly 20 years before. We used it to make a trip to New Orleans and from there to Galveston, seeing sights we had only heard of so far. Although we have since been in all the 48 states as well as Mexico and Canada, this first vacation was one of the best.

Fred Jr. and Florence

Many things happened as these four years went by. Fred and Florence were married in July of 1939, and in the Fall she went back with him to Manhattan to spend the last year of College. When he graduated the next Spring, Florence's father and mother went with us for the occasion, coming home by way of Independence and a visit with Nina's relatives. It was an enjoyable outing. Fred and Florence were soon settled at Pelican Rapids where he re-established the veterinary practice and he and I were referred to as Young Doc and Old Doc Hansen. Then in April of 1941 our first grandchild, Sharon Ann, was born. That was a great day for us.

Move to St. Paul—Sanitary Board and Stockyards

At the first of the year I was asked to come into the office in St. Paul to take over the position of veterinarian in charge of brucellosis control. We did not hesitate in accepting because my mother, although not an invalid, was finding it more and more difficult to keep up the house. Nina had expressed her willingness to help her and this solved the problem. So for a year and a half we were in Mother's house on Carter Avenue where Nina kept house and took care of her until her death in June of 1943. We then moved to an apartment complex in St. Paul called Highland Village.

For a couple of years before our 25th wedding anniversary, which should be in 1942, we made plans to celebrate the occasion with a trip to California and began a supposedly painless way of building up a travel fund by saving dimes. Whether or not it was painless, it was effective. People at home and the clerks and restaurant cashiers at the hotels where we were acquainted kept on shelling out dimes even after we were ready to quit. Then with the start of World War II and the gas rationing, our arrangement to stay with my mother, and a feeling that it would be more fitting to buy U.S. Saving Bonds than to go on a vacation, we postponed it. As compensation, we were rewarded by the arrival of our second granddaughter, Claudia Jo, on December 7th.

The work in the office of the Sanitary Board lacked the freedom of action, the personal contacts, the face-to-face confrontations, and the need for prompt decisions that had made the field work so interesting. After about a year and a half I gave it up and joined in a partnership with three of my friends who had taken over the cattle practice in the stockyards at South St. Paul.

This was a very well-paying business, but the work was harder and the hours longer than any I had known in country practice. There were few vacations and pleasure trips during the war years but we did manage a couple of times to take the train to Independence and also to Dubuque, Iowa, where Fred was stationed as a Captain in the Veterinary Corps of the Army. Florence and the girls were with him much of the time. They visited us often, with Sharon sometimes staying for a week or two.

At the end of the war, travel loosened up as if by magic. In the Winter of 1946 we took our first vacation in many years by driving to Florida. On the way home we went to Galveston for a few days and from there to Brownwood, Texas, where Fred had been recently transferred and was winding up his army service. Florence had gone down a week or so before, leaving the girls with her folks at Pelican Rapids and by pre-arrangement came back to Minnesota with us. After a good reunion with Florence's folks and the girls, we returned to St. Paul, rested and ready for work. It had been a wonderful vacation in every way. We had driven 5,748 miles and were looking forward to another trip.

The apartment at Highland Village was a comfortable and pleasant place to live but it was ten miles from the stockyards over what was, mostly, an open country highway. With one and often two trips a day this became quite a chore, especially in bad weather. So in the Spring of 1946 we bought a house in South St. Paul and moved on Mom's birthday. With getting settled and again having our own yard and garden to take care of, the Summer passed quickly. There was company, too, including Nina's sister Annie and her husband Soren. We took them on an outing to Duluth and the scenic drive on the north shore of Lake Superior and then across the state to see Fred and Florence and the girls at Pelican Rapids. It was fun.

The next Summer we took a vacation to the Black Hills and Yellowstone National Park. Our first sight of the Rocky Mountains, gleaming in the sunshine fifty or sixty miles away, was a sight we will never forget. Crossing the Big Horns the next day over secondary roads because a bridge was closed on the main highway gave us thrills we had never experienced before. Our destination was Billings, Montana, where we met friends and went with them for a few days at Yellowstone and a close-up view of the Grand Tetons. Returning home over the flatlands of North Dakota, it was hard to realize there could be so much difference in so few miles.

In October we were in Independence a few days but not on a pleasure trip. We attended the funeral of Nina's father. His was the first death on her side of the family in the thirty years we had been married.

The work at the yards was getting harder each year. One of the partners had died two years before, and in the meantime we had gotten by by hiring help or reshuffling the work schedules. Neither worked well. At the end of the year we dissolved the partnership, and in search of easier work, I applied to the Federal Bureau of Animal Industry for an appointment as a Veterinary Inspector, hoping there would be a vacancy in the stockyards at Kansas City. [This isn't clear.]

Denver, Colorado

As it happened there was no opening for an inspector in the stockyards in Kansas City, but there was one in Denver. So we sold the house, packed our things and moved, arriving in Denver the first part of April. It worked out real well. The work was pleasant, the climate wonderful, and we never tired of the mountains with their scenery and old historic places.

Our first visitors were Fred and Florence who came down to spend a few days in May. We, of course, went on mountain trips and one day drove up Pike's Peak as far as the road was open. We remember the motor getting hot on a steep climb and carrying water from a roadside stream in a candy box to refill the radiator. The road was blocked twelve miles from the top. We never did finish the climb.

Nina's mother was our second visitor. She enjoyed the mountains as much as we did and was interested in everything she saw. It was fun to have her along. High grades, steep drop-offs, hairpin curves, and even a huge boulder bouncing down a mountainside and stopping in the road a short distance ahead of us did not faze her. Grandma was a good traveler and happy whether feeding chipmunks on a mountain top, viewing the nothingness above timberline, or watching a "bilious" stream rushing downhill during the spring thaw. She visited us many times while we were in Denver and we were always glad to have her.

Other company came during the summer and we "explored" more and more with names such as Idaho Springs, Central City, Cripple Creek, and Leadville becoming common. We saw the Garden of the Gods, Mesa Verde, Ouray, and Silverton and drove the Trail Ridge Road above Estes Park. There was much to be seen in the Colorado Rockies.

In September we went to Pelican Rapids to welcome our third granddaughter, Ann Marie, who was born on August 22, 1948. On the way home we went by way of Minneapolis to see Olga, whose husband, Jennings, had died a few weeks before. We took her back with us for a short visit and a change of surroundings.

Our next trip was to Independence for Christmas. We drove but decided if we came again at that time of the year we would come by train. And so ended a very busy and interesting year with a pleasant holiday among the relatives.

The next year began as a continuation of the one before. In the early summer we spent a few days with Fred, Florence, and the girls at Pelican Rapids, returning again by way of Minneapolis. Company came and went, and we still enjoyed taking them on sightseeing mountain trips. There was one that could be made in two or three hours and was almost a must for visitors to Denver. It led up the gradually inclining highway to the Red Rocks Theater and from there to Lookout Mountain, which was the location of Buffalo Bill's grave and museum. The view included all of Denver, 2500 feet below and ten miles or so away, and stretched out over the rolling plains to the east as far as the eye could see. Just below was the town of Golden with houses that looked the size of match boxes. The road which led to it was fittingly called the "Lariat Loop." It was so steep and crooked and winding that once in awhile an uninitiated flatlander would close his eyes until the bottom was reached. It had all the thrills of mountain driving crowded into a few minutes.

When we visited Minnesota in the Spring, we found that Fred had become interested in government work and that he and Florence had both taken a liking to Colorado. So it was a pleasant surprise a few months later to learn that he had been appointed as a Federal Field Veterinarian and would be stationed at Fort Morgan, only 80 miles east of Denver. It meant a great deal to us to have the family so near. We visited forth and back on weekends and on special days and went on outings together, but seeing the grandchildren grow and having some part in their childhood activities was the most important of all.

For the three years and more, from November 1950 to March 1954, that we all lived in Colorado, we shared many things, including company.

Vacation Trip to California

In February of 1952 Mom and I finally took off on a trip to California which we had postponed ten years before. It was planned to be there for our anniversary on March third. On the way we stopped early one afternoon at Las Vegas with the thought we might stay a day or two. With Washington's birthday coming up the next day it seemed everyone else had the same idea; there just were not any rooms available. There was a town called Jean, 25 miles down the road, which was said to have several motels, so in the evening we left. There were no rooms at Jean or at Baker a couple or three hours farther on. By the time we reached Barstow, along about three o'clock, we had met so many headlights that we were ready to give up, park the car and wait for daylight.

Then we learned of a room at Fred Harvey's, over the Santa Fe Depot. These rooms had been built many years before, as in other depots along the line, to provide comfortable and respectable living quarters for the waitresses who worked in the Fred Harvey restaurants. Our room appeared to still have the original furniture. The bathroom was something by itself. The tub was huge, the lavatory was set in a heavy marble slab, the fittings were solid brass, and the toilet had a flush tank near the ceiling and a long dangling chain. A loudspeaker on the wall outside announced trains coming and going every so often, the bed shook as the trains came to shuddering stops below our window and the warning bell of a switch engine rang continuously. In spite of all the commotion, we slept well and were thankful to have a room and a bed. Breakfast was at an old marble counter in the lunchroom downstairs.

We stayed at Long Beach a week but drove into Los Angeles many times to see sights, take a bus tour and visit Knott's Berry Farm. There was no Disneyland at that time. We also called on an elderly couple who had been our neighbors in Denver. Our next stop was at San Diego where we spent a couple of days. The highlights there were the animals that could be seen from a small train that passed slowly in front of the cages, and a visit across the border to Tijuana. Then we stopped at Phoenix for two days and from there home. We felt that this vacation was worth waiting ten years for.

More Life in Denver

The big event of each year in Denver was the National Western Stock Show, which was held in January. Many of the city's activities were based on it. Since it was held at the stockyards, our work increased greatly at that time. Veterinarians from the field force were regularly called in to help us. Fred was usually included in this group. The family often came for part of the time, so it was a pleasant occasion for us all.

One summer all of us went on a peach-picking expedition on the Western slope. After getting settled in a hotel at Glenwood Springs, we drove to the orchards. The girls thought it was great fun to climb the ladders and pick the ripe fruit but not so much fun when they began itching from the fuzz. Bathroom showers soon took care of that. We came home loaded with peaches and other fruit and the memory of a good time.

Trip to New England

In 1953 Fred and Florence left the children with her folks at Pelican Rapids and the four of us left on a trip through Canada to the New England states, with New London, Connecticut, as our destination. Mom's oldest brother, Oak, had lived there since his service in the Navy during World War I. We entered Canada at Sault Ste. Marie on June 2nd which was the day Queen Elizabeth was being coronated. There were flags, bands and parades in every town and village we passed through.

At Ottawa we saw the Parliament Building and at Montreal a nightclub, busy in the afternoon, as well as an interesting ride on an open-air sightseeing trolley car with seats arranged in bleacher style so all had an equal view. As we drove south we passed through Montpelier, Vermont, with no idea that the next year the family would be living there and that we would be visiting them. When we got to New London, Oak and Mary had thought of many ways to entertain us. One day, following a plan that had been in the making for some time, we all took the train to New York City. We left New London long before daylight and arrived at the Grand Central Station in time for breakfast. Mom had studied travel guides quite thoroughly so became the director of our program. First we circled Manhattan Island, a distance of 35 or 40 miles, on a sightseeing boat with an announcer pointing out and telling of interesting places as we passed. After lunch at the Rockefeller Center we visited Greenwich Village, where artists were showing their works along the sidewalks. Then we rode a bus to Central Park where, without the time or inclination for a stroll, we did rest on a bench for awhile. We got home towards midnight, footsore and tired, but with the feeling we had seen as much in one day as anyone could absorb.-We agreed the day was one of the highlights of the trip.

Trip to the East

The following Christmas was the last we would have with the family at Fort Morgan because in March Fred was transferred to Montpelier, Vermont. In August Mom and I went back for a visit. The big event of that visit was a boat trip to Block Island about 30 miles out to sea. By the time we were halfway we might as well have been in the middle of the Atlantic. There was no sight of land, the waves were high, and the water very deep.

Mom and I left for Washington, D.C. for a night and part of a day. In New Jersey, we were in a fringe of a hurricane that struck the New England coast with a lot of damage to many places, including York Beach and New London, where we had recently been.

The American Legion was holding its national convention in Washington when we arrived, and rooms were at a premium. Luckily, we found a place in a small hotel quite a ways out. During our stay we would take a trolley into the city each morning and return by taxi at night. We used the lobby of the Willard Hotel as our headquarters and started our excursions from there. One of the most memorable was a bus ride to Mount Vernon and a leisurely trip back up the Potomac, resting in deck chairs on the deck of a boat. When we left we thought we had seen a lot of Washington, but it was only a drop in the bucket compared to the many sights Fred and Florence have shown us in later years.

This had been a wonderful trip and vacation but by the time we got back to Denver we were ready to settle down for a while. We had driven many miles over steep, winding narrow roads, especially in Virginia and West Virginia, that took much of the zest out of driving. Although there were some improved and modern toll roads on the , east coast, the Interstate Highways and Freeways of today had not yet been built.

The following summer two important changes took place. Fred was transferred to Oklahoma City, Oklahoma, where he became the Veterinarian in Charge of the Federal Disease Control program in the state. This was good news to us. Even though Oklahoma City was quite a drive from Denver, it was nothing compared to the distance to Montpelier.

Wichita, Kansas

The second change seemed like a bonus. In August I was transferred to Wichita, Kansas, to be in charge of the inspection at the stockyards there. In Mom's account of her childhood days she refers to the "Movin' Strahans." It seems by now she must have qualified as a "Movin' Hansen." With Wichita only a short half a day's drive from either Oklahoma City or Independence, we could not have asked for anything better. All of us, from all three places, appreciated the situation and for the next six years made good use of it.

The years at Wichita were gratifying. The work went well and the people with whom I worked were congenial and cooperative. We soon had friends and good neighbors as at other places we had lived. It was good to see Fred and Florence and the girls frequently and to be able to share some of the experiences with Sharon and Claudia as they went through the teens and with Ann as she approached that age. Company from Minnesota, including Olga and Florence's mother and father, came quite often. All of Mom's sisters and brothers and their families, including Oak and Mary, visited us. Grandma and some others came several times.

Grandma was always ready to go for a ride and enjoyed, especially, the trips to Oklahoma City. She was interested in everything she saw. There were no landmarks left at Orlando, Oklahoma, but she remembered this was where she and Grandpa Strahan, with Oak as a baby, had started from on the "run" when the Cherokee Strip was opened for settlement in 1893. In Perry, where Mom was born, there were plenty of landmarks left. Interstate 35 was not yet built and the highway passed the court house square in the center of the town. Mom and Grandma had a great time finding houses and places they both remembered from many years before. One day we stopped for lunch at a restaurant near the Square. There were a few middle-aged and elderly people at other tables and it was not long before a general conversation was in progress with Mom and Grandma in the middle. None of the participants, because of the generation gap, remembered Grandma but they recalled mutual acquaintances and common incidents. It was an interesting half an hour.

Denver Again

In January 1961 I was transferred back to Denver in charge of the Federal Inspection at the stockyards. Compared to Wichita it seemed we were a long way from both Oklahoma City and Independence.

In September, with retirement in mind, we bought a house in Independence just two doors from Soren's and Annie's, with whom Grandma made her home. The tenants were not anxious to leave, so we rented it to them for a year and set our retirement date for October 1st, 1962.

As it came closer to the time for our move, we spent a week in Independence cleaning and painting the house as best we could while Mom's brother, Joe, and his son Joe Jr, both carpenters, made repairs, installed cabinets, and improved the place as best they could. It looked good.

Retirement in Independence, Missouri

With our arrival at 1710 Harris Avenue, Independence, our Odyssey ended. We were back where we had started from in 1917, with memories of many experiences but with few regrets.

As we said, this story is a joint effort, so, even though I have done the writing, so far, it has been based on our combined recollections. Having reached the time of retirement it seems this is a good time to change places and for Mom to take over. So from now on she will continue the story.

Chapter 6

Sixty Years . . .. and More. Part Two, by Nina Strahan Hansen

"Sixty Years . . . and more, Part Two" is edited from a longer manuscript. What has been left out is primarily Nina's catalog of holidays spent with family and travelogue recounting routes and destinations of the periodic vacation trips taken by Fred and Nina during retirement years. These included regular visits with Fred's sister, Olga Hansen Litzenberg, either to see her in her home in Minneapolis or to travel other places with her. While these may be of interest to Fred and Nina's family, and aren't included here.

Retirement in Independence, Missouri

The Exodus from Denver to Independence, Missouri, was not painful to me. I had always hoped someday I could live closer to my mother. Nothing pleased her more than having us move close by. She was afraid she would not live long enough to see it.

After we were settled at 1710 Harris, all my relatives gave us a housewarming. Mama was never happier than being with all her children at our house. With a gift of money they gave us, we purchased a full-length mirror for my bedroom. Olga came by train from Minneapolis to spend a few days. It gave her a chance to meet all the relatives and see our little house.

Trip East

Our first trip was in June. We took Lynn with us and headed east to visit Oak and Mary in New London, Connecticut, then to Newport, Rhode Island, and saw all the old mansions that belonged to the "filthy rich" from New York City. From there we went to Cape Cod, Massachusetts. where we stayed a couple of days at

Provincetown. The shops and people were all quaint looking. You could easily tell the tourists from the natives. We stopped at Hyannis, but the Kennedy Compound was not open to the public. The stop at Plymouth rock was well worthwhile. We stood on the spot where the Pilgrims landed in 1620. The replicas of the Pilgrims' homes and the Mayflower II were interesting.

Frederic Hansen, Jr, Fred, Sr., Olga, Nina, Sophia, Jennings.

Our next important stop was at Niagara Falls. We took a tour of Goat Island and the trip on the "Maid of the Mist." It gave us some thrills. We were provided with "oilskins" or "slickers." The boat passed directly in front of the Falls and the spray was like a downpour. The boat did a lot of rocking in the turbulent water. We then drove across the Rainbow bridge to Niagara Falls, Canada where we spent a couple of days seeing the falls and scenic places. From the Seagram Tower, 325 feet high, we had a beautiful view of the falls and surrounding country and the two cities. On our way home we stayed in Hannibal, Missouri, the home of Mark Twain, and saw the historical places of "Tom Sawyer" days and a big river boat on the Mississippi River. We were gone three weeks and felt the trip had been well worthwhile.

In September Frederic was transferred to Washington, D.C. as a Senior Staff Veterinarian. We were happy for them but hated to see them leave Oklahoma City. It turned out good for them and also gave us a new place to visit.

November 1962

An invitation to spend Thanksgiving with Frederic and Florence gave us pleasure. On Armistice Day, November 11, 1963, we headed for Washington D.C. Being retired and with time on our hands, we spent three days on the way. On our way back to Springfield we stopped at Gettysburg, Pennsylvania, to see the historical battlefield. This was on November 22nd. While we were in an antique shop, the news of the assassination of President John Kennedy in Dallas, Texas, was announced. The next few days in Springfield we were all glued to the TV, watching and hearing about the events pertaining to his death, the funeral, and the transfer of the office to Vice President Lyndon Johnson. It was a hectic time. In spite of it we had a most enjoyable visit and trip.

Life in Independence

Dad and I played a lot of Scrabble during the winter months of 1964. We had the usual Saturday night hamburger suppers with Soren, Anna, Mamma, and Lynn. It was a nice way to end the weeks. Fred and Soren visited about Denmark and Soren's early life in America. He enjoyed having someone to tell the stories to. My folks didn't understand or care to listen to Fred's stories about veterinary work and stockyard regulations, so it was pretty hard on Fred not to have someone to unload on. I am sure there were times when Dad would have liked to visit with some old friends.

We celebrated Mama's 90th birthday on August 4th by taking her, Soren, Anna, and Lynne out to dinner. Mama's eyesight was failing and her hearing was impaired but she didn't miss out on anything. She was alert and always ready to go places.

Dad and I picked peaches at an orchard and did a lot of canning, including tomatoes from our garden. We got by this summer without air conditioners, which was not easy.

The middle of September we picked up Olga in Minneapolis and drove on to Aberdeen, South Dakota, where we stayed at the Holiday Inn. At Hecla and Houghton, we called on a few old friends of the Hansens, had a very good visit with the Tunbys, and went to the cemetery at Houghton where the Hansens are buried.

On Christmas Day [evening] we saw the famous Christmas Lights on the Country Club Plaza. So ended the year, a mixture of good times and sadness, but as the saying goes, "Into our lives some rain must fall."

January and February dragged along in 1969. By the time March arrived we were ready to celebrate our 52nd wedding anniversary with a trip to South Padre Island, Texas. We invited Oak and Lynne to go with us. Our first main stop was at Mission, Texas. We had lovely rooms at the Fontana Motel and stayed two days. Dr. and Mrs. Riemenschneider, old friends who lived there, had dinner with us one evening. In the morning we all went out to the Federal Laboratory where the doctor was studying diseases of sheep. One of his friends invited us to see his citrus grove and to help ourselves. Oak was quite excited about picking all the grapefruit, oranges, and lemons we could handle. The trunk of the car was so loaded, our luggage had to be put in the back seat on the way from Mission to South Padre Island. We drank orange juice and ate grapefruit until it came out of our ears.

San Padre Island was disappointing. The beach was covered with shells and the wind blew sand into our motel rooms. There was a constant roar from the angry waves and the weather was damp and gloomy. We spent one day going to Matamoros in Old Mexico. It was something different. The old beat-up taxi that brought us back across the border was something else. It gave us something to talk about.

We were gone three weeks, saw a lot, and the expense was not too great. The motels averaged $12.00 per day. It would have cost three times that much if we were to make the same trip now.

In April we were busy with the garden, house, and yard. There were a few family get-togethers. In June we took Olga on a trip to South Dakota. Olga and Dad saw a number of old friends in Hecla and Houghton. We had a turkey dinner at the Tunbys and visited the cemetery where the Hansens are buried. One evening the Tunbys came to our motel in Aberdeen and we had dinner together at the Downtowner Hotel. I thought, "Lobster Tails in South Dakota, no less." Olga enjoyed the trip as much as we did.

The first big excitement [of 1970] was in February. While Eveline and Ralph were in Florida, their house was broken into. The glass in the front door was broken and the police found a trail of blood leading up the street to where two boys lived. As far as we know, that was where the story ended. Nothing more was done about it.

We drove directly from Springfield to Minneapolis in time for Olga's Retirement Party given by the Nicollet Clinic, after fifty years. Following the party we took her on a whirlwind trip to Herman, Minnesota, to see Helen who was in a nursing home, on to Clinton, Iowa, to spend a couple of days with Cousin Sue and Frank, and then to Des Moines to visit Cousin John and Pearle. Olga went back to Minneapolis by train as we came home to find our garden full of weeds.

The first few weeks of 1971 were spent playing Scrabble, watching TV, and waiting for warmer weather. The big news was the landing of Alan Shepard and Edgar Mitchell on the moon. Then the big earthquake occurred in Los Angeles, California, where many people lost their lives with terrible damage in the area.

Blizzard

It was time to think about making a trip to see Olga again. It had been five months since she moved to the nursing home. So on the 9th of April [1972] we started for Minneapolis. The weather was not good but, foolishly, we hoped to run out of it. Instead, we ran into a real blizzard. We got as far as Bethany, Missouri, 98 miles from our house. The Good Lord was with us all the way. Credit goes to Dad for his good driving and many years of experience bucking snow drifts and blizzards in Minnesota. At a filling station in Bethany we learned the highway to Des Moines was closed. We were lucky to get the last motel room in town. It was a pretty sight to see the blinking sign, "Sunset Motel" as we pulled in the driveway. I sat in the car as Dad went to the office to register. The swirling snow and wind rocked the car as if someone was standing on the back bumper and jumping up and down. I rolled the window down to peek out and here came Dad, bucking the wind, holding on to his hat with one hand and carrying a pail of ice cubes in the other. What a welcome sight! It was a grand feeling to be in a warm comfortable room with a highball or two. The storm abated in the evening, the highway crews worked all night, and by the next morning we were on our way again. There were trucks, cars, and trailers stuck in snow drifts, especially at the overpasses, all the way to Ames, Iowa, with zigzag lanes plowed between and around them. Seventeen persons died in this storm. We were among the lucky ones.

Even though this was a hectic trip, we had a few good days with Olga and accomplished the things we had set out to do. We returned home "none the worse for wear" but would not care to go through the ordeal again.

First Plane Ride

During the rest of April and early May, we planted a garden and did the necessary things around the house. Then we treated ourselves by going to Washington, D.C., by plane. It was my first plane ride. It was thrilling but I was relieved when we landed. The plane trip home was uneventful. It was a nice way to travel.

Visit to Olga

The latter part of October [1973] we again went to Minneapolis to attend a big party at the Hilton Hotel in St. Paul at which Olga was given the "Harold Diehl" award by the Minnesota Medical Alumni Association for her outstanding work in the practice of her profession. Olga stood up to the occasion real well in the crowd of two hundred or more members. Cousin John and Pearle, from Des Moines, were there as well as several personal and family friends from Minneapolis.

More Life in Independence

In May [1975] we planted cantaloupe seed in our little garden plots. It was the finale of our gardening. There were vines all over the yard and lawn. The melons were plentiful, the relatives and neighbors helped us to get rid of them, and it was really fun while it lasted.

1975 was a good year with two exceptions. One was the death of [my sister's] daughter, June, in April. Then, in December, while [my brother and his wife] were in Florida, he had a stroke. These two events caused a lot of sadness. In a large family one has to accept bad things as well as good. Pain and sadness are a part of life. The things we cannot change we have to accept. We are thankful whenever we are able to be of help to those who are in need. I will admit it doesn't come as easy as it used to.

There was a lot of excitement on the first day of 1976. Eveline and Ralph's house was burglarized on New Year's Eve. Their neighbor called us to tell that he had found the bedroom window and basement door broken. The police came and questioned all the neighbors who had gathered. Dad and the neighbor boarded up the window and door. The next day we called the insurance agent who authorized repairs. The house had been ransacked with contents of drawers strewn all over the beds and floor, where it remained until the Websters returned the middle of February. It was a mess to come home to but they wanted to sort it over to see what had been stolen. It was a relief when Eveline and Ralph returned. Every night I worried about their house.

This story started on March 3rd, 1917. It seems like a good time to end it would be March 3rd, 1978. Looking back over the years we agree we have been very fortunate. We have had a wonderful life together and have a family of which we are very proud. Now, that Dad is eighty-two years old and I am eighty, we hope with God's help to have a few more years together to enjoy our children. I might add we have made plans already for the summer of 1978. Time will tell.

Independence Missouri

March 3, 1978,

Nina P. Hansen

Frederic W. Hansen

Chapter 7

To My Children, by Sophia Hansen

This story was a letter to Sophia's two living children, Fred Hansen Sr. and Olga Hansen Litzenberg. The transcription presented here is from the typed version made by Fred sometime after the death of his mother as it includes her death date. It was probably written by Sophia when she was nearly 80 years old, before Fred and Nina moved to St. Paul to live with her in January 1942.

"To My Children" has an unmistakable tone of melancholy beginning in the first sentence and amplified in the last two paragraphs. What she wrote about her children can be rightly interpreted as her depression speaking, and ought not reflect judgment on Olga and Fred. Sophia perhaps could not understand that they were busy pursuing their respective careers in human and veterinary medicine. This is probably easier for the 21st century American reader to understand than it was for a 19-20th century elderly Danish immigrant who felt alone and abandoned. Still Sophia, despite her basic Danish education and writing not in her native language, is remarkably articulate and shows herself to be a woman of considerable "strength and courage" (as she described herself in the fourth to the last paragraph). Consistent with her pious religious beliefs, though, she does not take credit for those admirable qualities, quickly adding that she drew those characteristics from sources unknown to her.

$\mathcal{C}. \mathcal{O}. \mathcal{N}_{yc}.$ COLUMBIA, DAK

Ole and Sophia Hansen – Wedding photo June 27, 1887, Hecla, Dakota Territory.

Rødekro, Denmark (Prussian-occupied Schleswig)

I have often wondered why I was born and permitted to live, the 9th child in a poorly regulated family. I was small and puny and physically poorly until the age of 19. My ambition always got the best of me as there was no strength. The country where I was born and grew up was a very poor country in every way. People were poor financially and not many got beyond a bare living.

Map of Denmark showing where Ole and his family came from, Slagelse, on the island of Zealand, and where Sophia grew up in Rødekro in southern Jutland.

Emigration from Denmark

At the time when I was twenty my health was pretty good and my ambition made me want to leave home and try some other country. By that time (1881) quite many people from my home surrounding had immigrated to North America and as a family consisting of man, wife, and four children, from 4 to 12 years of age were going, I persuaded my parents to let me go with them and out of their small savings they lent me money for the fare, to Detroit, Mich., where this family intended to live. We traveled 3rd class, had as much space for sleeping, dressing, and otherwise taking care of ourselves as an ordinary bedstead and we were all seasick most of the trip. We had to go to a kitchen for our food at mealtime and stand in line. Never will I forget standing in line among Polish, Italian, German, and many other nationalities, all of the poorer class of course, and see lice crawling on the clothing of many of them. Appetite with seasickness was too awful to try to remember, and the journey on that ship lasted 18 days.

Detroit, Michigan

I had planned to work in Detroit to earn money before going to Clinton, Iowa, where my brother Niels lived with wife and one child. Nobody who has not had experience can possibly imagine the feeling of starting doing housework in a third-class family[22] when one does not know anything about things in the house nor anything about the work and unable to understand or to speak to people. My main work was to take care of a boy of five who was feeble-minded. At times that boy was to be taken out for airing. It makes me shiver when thinking about all of that.

Clinton, Iowa

I wrote to my brother in Clinton for money to come from Detroit to Clinton and came alone. I was told that all I had to do was present my ticket and officials would see me safely through. By that time, however, I had lost faith in everybody but had also come to the point that I would not care what happened to me. In Chicago they transported me from one depot to another and placed me in the proper train but my mind was not sure until Clinton was reached. To travel in a strange land with barely enough money to pay fare is downright hardship. Should I ever see any person thus situated I would surely extend a helping hand.

I had learned dressmaking in my home, and after my experience with housework in Detroit that occupation did not appeal to me, but my brother Niels explained to me that housework was best for a

---

[22] Sophia is commenting that this was not a very well-functioning family.

while until I had learned something about the way people lived in this country. It was hard but the people I worked for were kind and considerate. There were three children in the family from 8 to 13, all eager to tell me names of objects and to ask me what the object was called in Danish. In no time the language became manageable but not without going through some difficulties which afterwards seemed amusing. I worked in Clinton three years, paid back what my parents had lent me, and also my brother, bought a full set of teeth and struck out for Chicago to become a dressmaker.

Chicago, Illinois

The first thing of real wonder I saw in Chicago was a streetcar running without horses to pull it. It was the first cable cars on State Street. Streetcars on all the other streets were run by mules or horses.

I rented a room in the homes of a Danish family and started to make dresses for private families for one dollar a day. Later after having equipped myself with a new system cutting chart and was more efficient, I could demand $1.50 a day. My work was agreeable but my health suffered. The gain made since leaving home (three years) was going fast and I became weak and miserable, sick in bed at least half the time. It was terribly lonely for me in Chicago and homesickness may have caused much of my illness. It is not easy to be absolutely alone, sick and nothing but one's work to depend upon. After working two years in Chicago or less, a Danish woman living near where I roomed and boarded engaged me to make dresses for her daughters and herself. She noticed my poor health and told me a friend of hers had been similarly afflicted and that she had gone west to Dakota and was now well. She concluded by saying "I have a dear aunt out there. She would be glad to have you come to her." This woman, Mrs. Schmidt, was a cousin to the man I married a couple years later, but at the time it was simply a casual remark. But that aunt of Mrs. Schmidt's had a son who on his way to visit relatives in Denmark was introduced to me, and in a year's time we were married in Dakota, and the aunt became my mother-in-law, and lived with me until her death in 1906.

Ole P. Hansen in Dakota Territory

When Dakota Territory was opened for settlement, a great many people disposed of homes and property in states farther east and filed on free land there. The vast plains were attractive to farmers. They could begin ploughing at once, which was greatly in contrast to the process in other places where timber had to be removed before cultivation could begin—great saving in time and labor. It must have been about 1880 when Ole with his mother and two younger brothers came from Michigan out there to build a home and were given free land, which, after complying with certain laws they received proper title to.

Ole's land was the farthest north of any settlers at that time and the nearest town was Columbia, twenty miles south, and that was as far as the Northwestern railroad was built at that time. It must have taken a lot of courage and strength to haul by horse, mule, or ox team everything they needed, lumber, nails, groceries, coal, seed-grain, farm implements. They even had to go to Columbia to get plow shares sharpened.

In 1884 the railroad was built north as far as Oakes, North Dakota, now. A railroad town was started 3½ miles north of Ole's farm and was welcomed by the settlers. The town was named Hecla[23] and like towns in a new country had its full share of all imaginable vice. There were people who intended to get rich without working, which always is the case in a new country town, but there were also honest pioneers who had a hard time of life. This town never grew big. Until this day it has only 400 or 500 inhabitants.

The land for miles and miles around was flat. Neither tree, hill,

---

[23] Dakota became South Dakota and North Dakota on November 2 1889. Hecla is in Brown County, South Dakota very near to the North Dakota border.

nor lake anywhere near. James River runs about a mile and a half west of Hecla and the same distance from Ole's farm. At that time when settlers first came to Jim River Valley the river held high hopes for the pioneer farmers in regard to transportation, as steamboats carrying freight as far north as Columbia were in operation several years. That hope of cheap freight blasted.[24] The river dried up some seasons so people could drive across without a bridge.

Hecla, Dakota Territory

Ole and I were married on June 27th, 1887. Raising wheat on these vast prairies without a root or a stone to interfere with ploughing or seeding had given farmers hope of success as the land was new and yielded good returns year after year without rest or fertilizing of any kind. But our land was sandy and in 1889 we had a lot of wheat destroyed early in the spring by wind storms. We, like most farmers, had no cattle or stock of any kind to fall back on. We did not have harvest enough that year to pay what we had borrowed to get along with during the summer. We had five bad years, working harder and getting poorer each year. Had a crop in 1892 but then more bad years.

Here we began to trade horses for cattle and in a short time we had stock of different kinds, sheep, cattle, horses. We began to get on our feet, and as our hopes and courage had never failed, we felt now that we could make a living for our family. We had now three children, all born during the years of hardship. Ole's mother made her home with us until her death in 1906, at the age of 84. She often spoke of her first years in Dakota when she kept house for her boys. How they would leave her in the morning alone in their claim shanty to go twenty miles to Columbia for provisions. No road but wagon tracks over the prairie and the prairie looked so endless. Indians were prowling though not hostile, but Grandmother was afraid to be

---

[24]I.e. That hope of cheap freight didn't work out.

alone over a mile from neighbors. She said she looked at her disappearing boys as long as she could see them and offered up a prayer for their return. I can easily imagine how she felt.

Ole worked hard and did not hire help when we could do the work ourselves. I had learned to drive horses and also to milk cows, and as Grandmother was always ready to take care of the children, I filled the place of a hired man a good deal. Grandmother loved the children dearly so it was a pleasure to her to do things for them and they appreciated her always. How I had the strength and courage to do what I had to do has always been a mystery to me.

Ole was devoted to his family at all times. At times when difficulties would arise, he was always ready to make the best of matters and comfort us all. He and I often expressed our feeling in a declaration like this: We shall not care how hard we have to work while the children are small if we can only feel that in time we can give them the education they want and they have in life what we have been denied. Our wish in that direction was granted. God was good to us, and we were able and glad to give our children a chance to make a way for themselves. We without a doubt could have done different at times but we did as well as we understood and more pure and unselfish love no parent have had for their children than we had for our children. We were often misunderstood but the motives were never at fault.

While I am unspeakably lonely and feel neglected and set aside by my children, I never feel bad that Ole is not here any more. When meeting with disappointment it often comes to my mind that he would have met similar disappointments had he been here and I should be glad that he is not here any more. My constant prayer is for wisdom and understanding to live and do the will of God while my life on earth shall last.

Chapter 8

West-Fever, by John G Thomsen

John G Thomsen was the only son of John Thomsen, first cousin of Fred Sr., and nephew of Sophia. In this essay John quotes from Chapter 3 in this book and more extensively from a birthday gift written in pencil in longhand by Sophia to help John G know more about his father. The text for that will be found in a manuscript in preparation for publication. "West-Fever" was written for presentation to the Prairie Club, Des Moines, Iowa, on March 30, 1984. This was a group of perhaps 30-40 men of many professions (law, medicine, business) which met monthly for dinner and a scholarly talk. On a rotating basis member shared on various subjects mostly outside of their areas of professional life. The standards for an interesting and academic paper were high and the presentation required extensive preparation. Two other Prairie Club papers were on medical quackery and the diaries of Samuel Pepys.

The one hundred years prior to 1914 saw the movement of approximately fifty million people from Europe, the largest single migration in the history of the human race. For most of those people the destination was America.

This migration was not a sudden or spectacular mass movement as has sometimes occurred in response to military conquest; it was a slow, gradual departure of individuals, each responding to circumstances which led to the decision to emigrate. An "emigration fever" had spread through Europe; Rolvaag, in his

Giants in the Earth, called it "West-fever".[25] Young people, especially, faced the decision: to emigrate or to stay.

Each of us is a transplanted European; only the time of the transplantation and the number of persons involved vary. Regardless of the country or countries of origin of our antecedents, the crossing of the Atlantic is an event common to our heritage.

My parents were two of the approximately 300,000 persons who emigrated from Denmark between 1864 and 1914. Their experiences against the background of the emigration from that small country of only 2 million people can be seen as a small sampling of the movement from all of Europe. Obviously, such an account cannot be thought of as typical for other countries; infinite variations of time and circumstance would make that impossible. But in many ways their experience can suggest the general experience.

One can hardly examine the experiences of the first-generation Americans without considering how their children, the second-generation Americans, were affected by the transplantation. The immigrants, in spite of their best efforts, could never entirely cease to be European, nor could they become totally American in every detail of speech or custom or attitude. No doubt these influences continue in a "ripple effect" of decreasing intensity through the following generations, but it is by the second generation that they are most strongly felt. For this reason, it seems necessary to include some of my own recollections and impressions, particularly from childhood.

This account is not of the early pioneers, log cabins, sod house, and related hardships; it deals with a later period. These immigrants

---

[25] Rolvaag, O.E. *Giants in the Earth*. Harper and Row, New York. Perennial Library edition, 1965. p 219.

came to a young and rapidly expanding country, but one with towns laid out, houses and business establishments already constructed.

I have observed that immigrants tended to choose countryside similar to that which they left. The Finns and Swedes settled beside small lakes in forests of pine and birch in northern Minnesota. Germans found the rolling, green hills of Wisconsin to their liking. On the other hand, Norwegians, accustomed for centuries to farming small fields of nearly vertical land, seemed happy to find the large, flat lands of the central plains and appeared to have no further desire to live in the mountains. My parents came from a flat country with low, thick-walled, whitewashed houses and poor roads; they came to a flat country with wooden houses and poor roads.

But, before we examine the experiences of my parents, let us look back at the circumstances which brought on and sustained the great event.

I

Studies on migration in general have been based on the concept of "push" and "pull", the circumstances in the place of origin which would bring pressure to leave and the attractions which might encourage one to go elsewhere. These factors as they apply especially to Denmark have been carefully analyzed by Kristian Hvidt, a Danish scholar of the social history of the emigration, and this background is based in great part on his writings[26]

Developments on both sides of the Atlantic during the last century encouraged the migration. The population in the rural areas of Denmark had outgrown the land's ability to sustain it. Movement

---

[26] Hvidt, Kristian, *Flight to America: The Social Background of 300,000 Danish Emigrants.* New York: Academic Press, 1975, and Hvidt, Kristian. *Danes Go West, A Book about the Emigration to America*. Rebild: Rebild National Park Society, Inc., 1976.

to the towns and cities was impeded by a lag in industrial development, and there was a high rate of unemployment at all levels. On this side of the Atlantic, a rapidly developing nation needed people and could offer them a future which they could only dream of in Europe. Thus, the mass migration played a role, along with the industrial revolution and rapid capitalistic expansion, in the development of this country.

There were stirrings of unrest in Europe in the late 1700s. Then came the Napoleonic Wars, followed by a period of economic crises, disorganization and poverty which persisted through much of the 19th century. Denmark was primarily an agricultural land, a land of farms and small villages. People living near the coast were more aware of the outside world, but inland, in earlier days, there had been little movement beyond the parish boundaries. But gradually, with improved roads and other means of communication and with the stimulus that came from compulsory education, the possibility of a better life became a vision for more and more people, a concept which has been termed "social buoyancy".

There were several directions in which this upward pressure might lead; one was land ownership. With land reforms of the late 1700s the village collectives had been modified so that farms were established in the outlying fields and ownership of the land by individual farmers became possible. But the farms, already small, continued to be sub-divided until, by the last half of the 19th century, this was no longer possible. At the same time, an increased birth rate and decreased infant mortality led to larger families. This was especially true in farm worker families where, as Hvidt puts it: "This resulted from the motto that children are the poor man's wealth, and there is little doubt that farm laborers actually saw child-breeding as an investment since at that time children could be sent to work at an early age and help increase a family's income."[27] So, if the small family farm passed to the oldest son, there were usually several others, sons and daughters, for whom the possibility of land ownership did not exist.

A second possibility was to leave the countryside for the towns and cities, but there, as in the country, jobs were scarce. In the country, even in summer, unemployment levels often reached 40% or more, and, at best, the prospect was that of a lifetime as a poorly paid farm hand or servant, a lifetime of menial work for others. Again, quoting Hvidt: "The 1849 constitution, which laid the foundation of democracy in Denmark, only added to the humiliation of these landless peasants by denying them the right to vote unless they had households of their own."[28] Servants were required on penalty of fine or imprisonment to carry and abide by the rules of a "conduct book" and to report to the authorities on entering or leaving a parish. Hvidt adds: "No wonder they searched desperately for ways to break loose from their social yoke. The help was to come in the form of enlightenment and new means "of transportation such as railways and steamships."[29]

An additionally "push" factor which applied to large numbers of men, including my father, was the prospect of military service in the German army. A decisive military defeat by Prussia in 1864 had left some 200,000 Danes living under German rule in the border province or Slesvig. As they approached the age of compulsory service, many left—they evaded the draft.

With the use of a computer, Hvidt recently analyzed data from records kept by the Danish police, information about each person who emigrated from Denmark beginning in 1868. There emerges

---

[27]Hvidt, *Danes Go West.* p 29.

[28] Op cit p 32.
[29] Op cit.

wat he calls a pattern of "Migratory Selection". Again quoting Hvidt: "(It is) . . . a distinct patter with respect to the emigrant's age, sex, last residence, and occupations. It should be possible to say, with reasonable certainty, that in Denmark in the 1880's a young man aged 18-20 year, employed as a farm hand (in a certain locality) . . . would be likely to emigrate. A certain pattern of emigration has been established that indicates which tensions in the socio-economic condition s of Denmark induced particular sections of the population to leave home."[30]

What we have been considering up to this point are the "push" factors, the factors which determined that certain people, and not others, would emigrate. These were the most powerful factors, those which set the population moving. They were chiefly economic.

"Pull" factors, though less important, can be thought of as accelerators or catalysts of a process already begun. Personal contacts, such as letters from relatives or friends already in America, were strong influences. Sometimes money or prepaid tickets were sent. There was a shortage of young women in the United States; sometimes a man returned to find a wife; occasionally there was a proposal by mail.

A new profession, that of Emigration Agent, was born; there was active solicitation of passengers by competing steamship companies and railroad companies. Commissions were paid at all levels on both sides of the ocean as agents in Europe signed up emigrants and agents in the United States sold prepaid tickets to immigrants to be sent back to their relatives. Railroad companies solicited people, not only as passengers but to help build the expanding railroad system and to populate the country along their new routes. Some states, notably Wisconsin, Minnesota and Nebraska, joined with private interests to attract people. Agents with pamphlets went to

---

[30] Op cit.

the Scandinavian countries to attract people to southern Minnesota and later to Dakota. The expansion of agriculture, mining and industry required people, and strong efforts were made to attract them.

But it was the Homestead Act in 1862 which was to provide the greatest pull; it offered free to anyone over 21 years 160 acres of land to be deeded formally after five years of residence and making a farm out of the prairie. It was, as Hvidt ut it: "The Homestead Act (which) opened the gates for the human flood across the Atlantic".[31]

So they came, leaving the culture their forefathers had evolve over many centuries, leaving parents and family, often without real expectation of being reunited.

II

My father, John Thomsen, was born in 1864 to Danish parents in Slesvig, that part of the disputed border territory alternately ruled by Denmark and Prussia for several centuries. His lifetime, 1864 to 1923, coincided almost exactly with the period of German control which began with the Peace of Prague in 1864 and ended after World War I with the restoration of northern Slesvig to Denmark in 1920.

My father was the youngest of eleven children; seven sons and four daughters were reared on a small farm, only 25 or 30 acres. Three of the sons and three of the daughters emigrated. One of the daughters returned; one of the sons was heard from a few times, then disappeared. One sister, Sophia Hansen, had emigrated a year before my father. A few quotations from her written reminiscences (reference no. 4) will help to set the scene in the Danish countryside from which they came: "We kept a few cows and sheep and one horse. The land was of extremely poor quality and the surroundings

---

[31] Op cit p 110.

unattractive. It was far from school and far from church and everything worthwhile but we children did not realize our disadvantages, it was home to us… the boys worked out summers coming home to attend school winters until they were confirmed. After confirmation they did not go to school any more but made their own living. . . We had a swamp where peat fuel was made each summer and the (younger) children were made useful setting peat up to dry or (loading it) on a wagon to be hauled home (into) a shed or . . . Father would haul small, one-horse loads to the city . . .about eight miles, to sell…"

Aunt Sophia writes further that in the summer before my father was confirmed, at the age of 14 1/2 . "He was considered too big a boy to go to school . . . so he was hired out to a very small farmer near our home. The farmer and family were inferior people in every way and with poor food and senseless management the place was truly undesirable. John was helped to stand it by being able to come home and be comforted and encouraged by Mother. To quit a place before the time was up was looked upon as a disgrace . . . . The Following winter John was prepared for confirmation which took place in the spring. That spring John started out to take care of himself. He hired out to a farmer in our vicinity where he was hired to be man of all jobs (Stordreng)". Largely due to his skill in handling horses he soon rose to the position of foreman (Avlskarl), a job he continued until he reached military age.

Aunt Sophia continues: "We were under (the) German government at that time and every able-bodied young man was forced to serve three of his precious years in the army. The cruel treatment, poor food, idleness and temptation ruined many nice young men and made worthless people of them for the rest of their lives. Many left their homes and came to America to avoid military service, but the government made it hard for them to get away. They had to take the law into their own hands and desert, (risking) the consequences which would be severe punishment and double time service if they were caught. John took the risk, (preferring) anything to being a German soldier. He had money enough to buy a ticket to America and in order to get (a) passport . . . went to visit our brother Hans in Denmark. (He) stayed there the required time that Denmark demanded to issue a (passport) and then (in 1882) took (a) ship for America.

"He was headed for Clinton, Iowa where our brother, Niels lived. All would have gone well enough, but a few days out at sea something happened to the ship so it had to be brought into Hamburg, Germany for repair. Here the passengers were ordered to leave the ship; it would be three days before it could sail again. On leaving the ship each one of the passengers had to show (his passport) and as John's would show he was a German subject his case would be looked into by military officers who were looking out for deserters. When John told about (it), the fear and anguish he experienced, he failed to find words to explain how he felt." The disembarkation and re-boarding were, however, successfully carried out through a ruse involving the re-use of the passport of a fellow-passenger of similar appearance.

He arrived in Clinton, nineteen years old, able to speak German as well as Danish but with no knowledge of English. Again, from Aunt Sophia's recollections: "He was tired from the trip, homesick and overly anxious to get to earn money. So, after resting at Niels's (home) a short time, he started out afoot and alone to look for work among the farmers. He found work with "a farmer at Low Moor near Clinton . . . soon gained the friendship of a son of the house . . . . (and with) his help . . . mastered English very rapidly". During his three year period "he met and fell in love with a school teacher, a daughter from a neighboring farm . . . Soon after she and John became engaged her health began to fail. Her parents made it unpleasant for their daughter and her lover by proving that they did not approve of this young Scandinavian whom their daughter had chosen to become her husband. When (she) died, John mourned deeply and the fact that her parents completely ignored him made it harder to bear. Thus he was made acquainted with grief early in life."

In about 1888, he and two friends pooled their savings and went to Ida County as what Aunt Sophia described as a "cowboy trio". In her words: "They planned to take cattle to herd for others and to get the benefit of the increase in number and weight of as much stock as they could buy. Luck went against them however. The grass dried up for want of rain . . . disease infested their herd so they lost all they had invested and were in debt besides. . . . It was during that experience that John fully decided to become a veterinarian. It seemed to him so unworth6 to see nice young cattle get sick and die and he was unable to do anything about it. When he told me about it he said: 'even if it takes till I am fifty years old I will not give up until I am a veterinarian'."

After further work as a farm hand in Ida County and in Dakota, he returned to Clinton, where, in 1889 he became naturalized citizen, renouncing his allegiance to the King of Denmark. He had obtained a position as coachman for a well-to-do family thus enabling him to save money and to attend night classes to improve his English and to broaden his basic education. In 1895 he achieved his goal by graduating, with honors, in veterinary medicine from the Ontario Veterinary College in Toronto.

His next stop was Brown County, South Dakota to visit his sister, Sophia, and her husband and to collect a graduation present, a horse. With the horse and a newly-purchased cart he reached Estherville, in Northern Iowa, the place he had chosen to begin practice. His practice there was disappointing, and he soon moved to another smaller town in Emmet County, Armstrong.

His first marriage was in 1898 to a young woman, also an immigrant from Denmark, whom he had known in Clinton and with whom he had continued to correspond. During the next years the practice slowly increased, and it became possible to remodel an old house and to erect a building, referred to as "the barn", in which to conduct his practice. There were no children; their marriage ended with his wife's death of a chronic heart ailment, in 1913.

III

My mother was born on a farm in Denmark in 1888, the second of ten children. After her mother's death and her father's remarriage, she, from the age of nine or ten, found her energies occupied in assisting her step-mother with household duties and the care of the younger siblings, who were born at frequent and quite regular intervals. Her education was limited to the eighth grade, the usual extent of formal schooling, especially in rural areas, at that time.

At an early age, she, in a literal translation of the Danish expression, "went out to earn". Her "conduct book", the legally required document for servants, was issued to her over the signature and seal of the parish minister just four days after her confirmation at the age of fourteen and records her subsequent movement from one parish to another.

In 1913, and the age of twenty-five, she made the decision to travel to America. She had been encouraged by a maternal uncle who had emigrated and lived in northern Iowa. Her stated plan was to stay for five years, hoping during that time to have earned enough money to find a better life in Denmark on her return.

IV

My parents' first meeting was in 1913, when my mother, newly arrived from Denmark, took employment as a housekeeper in my father's home, soon after he had become a widower. I have no knowledge of how their romance evolved; it never occurred to me to ask. But it appears not to have been a sudden thing since it was not until 1919, six years later, that they were married. During that time, while continuing in the role of servant, she had improved her language skills and become further adapted to the customs of the new country.

I was their only child. I have no recollections of my father, who died in 1923, two years after I was born. But I do have a mental picture of him, partly based on my mother's reminiscences, partly on written recollections of my Aunt Sophia's son, Fred Hansen,[32] who spent parts of two years working with my father as an apprentice veterinarian, and partly on artifacts left in the "barn".

From these sources I conclude that he was a gregarious man, filled with enthusiasm for life and especially thrilled with the freedom, the opportunities, and the advantages which he had found in America. He had acquired an education which would have been impossible for him in his homeland; he had acquired some land, something which would have been unthinkable for one of his station in Denmark; he could vote, and he had witnessed the rapid industrialization and technological advancement in his new country. In terms of direct participation in the results of those achievements it must have seemed to him that he had moved ahead in time at least one generation. He was fascinated by gadgets and was quick to respond to ads for a variety of things; I remember finding such things as what must have been the earliest ball-point pen and a complicated wheel lock for an automobile among other unidentifiable devices, findings which I have sometimes thought of as part of the "archeology of the barn".

In the early days of his practice, calls were made with horses and a cart or buggy, replaced in winter by a sleigh. The "barn" was equipped with three box stalls for the horses; it also housed an elaborate operating table for horses, an upright device to which the animal was first strapped and then tilted by a wonderful array of cranks and pulleys to the horizontal position. It was an unusual

---

[32]See Chapter 3.

device, built especially for him, but it was apparently too much trouble for regular use.

A series of early Model T Fords finally replaced the horses. But there had been an earlier car, one described in some details by Fred Hansen: "Uncle John's car at that time was an Imperial Roadster. It was big and strong and flashy. With its full leather upholstery, with the brass-wear polished and the exhaust sounding in perfect sequence it was an impressive vehicle. It had a pair -- -the only ones I have ever seen – of steel-studded outer tires which would send a shower of sparks remindful of twin comets. The car did have a few weak points too. The most serious of these was the almost and sometimes total lack of braking power . . . . Behind the wheel of the Imperial, Uncle John could be likened to (a) knight of old, mounted on a fiery, half-tamed charger and ready to accept any challenge or to offer a few of his own. At a time when the expression, "Forty miles an hour", denoted an unbelievable highway speed he did not hesitate to drive the speedometer needle to the top figure of 60 and push it some on the second go 'round. It was not unusual to see him pass up a farm driveway and then battle the car to a halt a quarter of a mile beyond. There were probably some who described Thomsen as a reckless driver. On this I shall not comment but shall only add that to enjoy the ride his passenger needed a streak of recklessness of his own. . . . The Ford which replaced the Imperial did not give him much of a thrill. He drove it moderately but with no affection".[33]

Further quoting Fred Hansen: ". . . he was in the middle of a deal with a firm in Germany for an 'aero-plane' when World War I cut the transaction off. He still talked about a plane and had what he knew was a far-fetched idea of a pair of rails extending out and upward from the upstairs of the barn to help boost the machine into the sky. It was far-fetched, of course, but at that time the description of a helicopter would have been equally fantastic. This was when

[33] Op cit.

authorities on aviation maintained that the extreme load limit of any plane would be, for all time, a pilot and one passenger".[34]

I have reason to believe that he as a skillful veterinarian, and by the time of his death he had developed a sizable large animal practice. When he died, in 1923 at the age of sixty, he left the property consisting of the house and the "barn", some farm property, substantially mortgaged, and a 1917 Franklin touring car. In his bank box I discovered, many years later, 1000 shares in Mount Masonic Mining Company, Salt Lake City Utah, 25 shares in The Iowa Development Company, investors in the Acme Oil and Gas Co. (oils wells in Franklin County, Kansas), and a Cooperative Membership in the Gopher Tire and Rubber Co. of Minneapolis.

I have every reason to believe that, despite the 24-year age differenced, my parents' marriage was a happy one. There was always the same deep sigh as my mother left his gravesite after placing decorations. Though I didn't think of it then, I'm sure my father's shadow continued to influence my mother's attitudes and actions throughout my boyhood, probably during her entire life. To her great credit, she was able, by determination and careful management, to keep possession of the mortgaged farm property through the depression, something that eluded many others, and finally, in 1939, to pay the last of the mortgages.

V

'Over the hills and far-away to grandmother's house' was a song we sang in school, a song, that, had I given it thought, had little first-hand meaning for me. We made only one trip to grandmother's house during my childhood, 1200 miles by train and a 3,000 mile ocean voyage. But we stayed several months, long enough for me to forget, at the age of three, all of the English I had known and to become as fluent in Danish as 3 year-olds become. Those skills were again quickly reversed when we returned. Isolated events in

---

[34] Op cit.

177

preparation for the trip and during the trip are among my earliest recollections: traveling with friends in a curtained car to the county seat to obtain the passport, a sailor suit bought for the occasion, the marvels of travel by train and steamship. I am still thrilled by the sound and vibration of a foghorn.

We left home in the spring of 1924, a few months after my father's death. For my mother it must have been a timely visit with her family after a decade abroad, an opportunity for support in her bereavement, and a chance to show off her child. She had been the only member of her family to emigrate, and no doubt there was discussion and encouragement from them for her to return to live in Denmark. Though there was always a strong affection for her family and her native country, I am sure she never seriously considered leaving her new country. When she died suddenly, in 1960, while on a return visit to Denmark, the question of whether she would not have chosen to be buried there was raised by her family. For me, there was no difficulty in that decision; I knew she would wish to be buried beside my father in the small country churchyard in northern Iowa.

VI

The influences on me, as a second generation American, came not only from the town in which I spent my childhood, but from another small town, seven miles away.

The first, Armstrong, had been founded and populated almost entirely by people of English-speaking origins: Scottish, Irish and English. Some of them were immigrants, but many were the second and third generation descendants of families which had first settled along the Atlantic seaboard, people who had made a secondary westward migration. **A comparison of surnames and places of origin in the 1880 and 1900 census roles shows clearly that it was only by the latter decades of the century that Scandinavians and Germans arrived in that community.**

By contrast, the people of Ringsted, the second town, were predominantly of Danish origin. The significance of this aspect of the western movement is nicely summarized by Marcus Lee Hansen: "We are beginning to see that the Mississippi Valley was for fifty years the frontier of Europe as well as of the Eastern states and that it reacted upon England, Germany and Scandinavia with a force comparable to that which it exerted on Atlantic America . . . the hundreds of immigrant communities in America that formed the human connecting link between the old world and the new . . . the millions of personal contacts that brought humble public opinion on both sides of the Atlantic so close together."[35]

In Armstrong, I grew up among Stewarts, Campbells, Ogilvies, Churchills, Matthews, Duffeys, Cannons, and Knights. Ringsted was a town of Jensens, Petersens, Hansens, Christensens, and Nelsens.

It was to the home of Nels Peter Nelsen, my mother's uncle, that she had come when she arrived in the United States, and, in the early days at least, he must have served somewhat as a surrogate father for her. And, though we visited them infrequently, it was this family with eight sons and daughters together with their spouses and children which comprised the nearby 'family' for us. If immigrants can be thought of as having a 'support system' beyond the old country, then the support system for my family was in Ringsted on my mother's side and Clinton, Iowa and Saint Paul, Minnesota on my father's. (Aunt Sophia and her husband, Ole P. Hansen, moved from South Dakota to Bird Island, Minnesota in 1909 and to St. Paul in 1913 or 1914). Occasional visits to Clinton or Saint Paul and packages bearing those postmarks at Christmas-time were among the highlights of my childhood. But it was during visits to Ringsted that my most intense exposure to things" Danish" occurred. It such a community, immigrant wives commonly spoke little or no

---

[35]Hansen, Marcus Lee. *The Third Generation*. (In *Children of the Uprooted*--- edited by Oscar Handlin.) George Braziller, New York, 1966. p 270

English. Business dealings involving English were carried out by the men; dealing with grocers and other local merchants could easily be conducted in Danish, so the incentive to learn the new language was not great. Understandably, children born to immigrants in that setting learned Danish at home as their first language.

Ringsted had two Danish Lutheran churches. One was within the town and had services conducted in English, serving the needs of those who favored more rapid Americanization for themselves and their children the other, a mile from the town (and between the towns of Ringsted and Armstrong), was a typically Danish church; tombstones with Danish inscriptions stand in its adjacent cemetery. It was in this church that my parents had at least a nominal membership; it was here that Danish traditions and language were preserved. In its earliest days, I suspect that the only service was in Danish; within the period of my memory there were two services, the first in Danish and the second in English.

I can recall attending church services there only a few times. The sermons, given by an old-fashioned appearing man with a white ecclesiastical ruff, seemed endless to me. On one occasion I found an excuse to slip out early and wait in the car. I was soon engaged in conversation with someone I took to be an older man – probably about twenty-five – who told me that he had come for a week-end visit with his mother but that he too had found the service boring and had seen his chance to leave. It was a meeting, as they say, of kindred souls. He told me that he was from a larger town someplace in Iowa and that he was in the "shoe game". I still think of anyone connected with the sale of shoes as being in the "shoe game".

In the Danish-styled 'gymnasium' which adjoined this church, a parochial school was conducted each summer after the closing of public school. During two summers when I was about nine or ten, I attended, in response to my mother's persuasion, the first of two three-week sessions, that given in Danish. Most of the instruction, as I recall it, was given by women, most likely of the second generation, women who had learned Danish as their first language at home and spoke it well; subjects covered, as I remember, were Bible study and readings relating to Danish history and folk literature. With the exception of baseball and classic Danish gymnastics after classes were finished, I'm sure I regarded the three week period as an unnecessary and unwanted delay in getting on with summer. For my mother, it may have allayed some feelings of conflict in her loyalties.

In relationship to Ringsted, living in Armstrong, so far as things Danish were concerned, was like living in an outpost. Language adaptation was not a major problem for first and second generation people of English-speaking origins, the English, Scottish, and Irish; no doubt there were differences in accents and usage, especially in the first generation, but, since their basic language was the language of the new country, they faced one less obstacle to adaptation than did those from non-English-speaking countries.

I believe that my parents' goal was to adopt the English language and to become Americanized without delay. Most of the publications received in our home were in English: the Des Moines Register, the Sunday Chicago Herald-Examiner, The Armstrong Journal, The Ringsted Dispatch, and The Literary Digest. But, for a time at least, subscriptions to two Danish language periodicals continued: Dannevirke, and Kvinden og Hjemmet (The Woman and The Home), both published, I believe, in Cedar Falls.

I have reason to believe that my father acquired greater fluency in English than my mother; he had, of course, been in the United States for 21 years before she arrived, had taken courses in English, and had earned his degree in an English-speaking school. English was the language of our household with the exception of those expressions which were needed on short notice, such as: 'do you have to go to the toilet?' or 'Are you going to vomit?' Telephone conversations with Danish-speaking friends or relatives were also carried out in Danish.

I was aware that my mother had certain peculiarities in English usage and pronunciation, but I did not from the beginning think of her as having an accent. Of course, she did, and one incident in particular stand out in my memory. She would sometimes coach me in preparing my Sunday School lesson and I can tell you that in my town and in the English-speaking church which we attended, when you meant to say something about Joseph in Egypt and it came out "Yosef in Aegypt" before your seven-year-old classmates, you took on a burden which you would carry for a while.

Emigration involving a language change exacts a toll. On later visits to her family in Denmark, my mother found that she no longer spoke Danish fluently; she had lost some of her skills, and the language in her native land had undergone change. So, she was in a position of being fluent in neither language, one of the by-products of the great uprooting.

Inevitably, the customs of our home were influenced by our origins. There was a year-round emphasis on Scandinavian foods, among others, homemade rye bread; traditional foods such as kringle, almond cookies and 'pepper nuts' appeared at Christmas-time. Homemade wine, provided by Danish friends, was served on special occasions during that season, and, in accordance with European tradition, I was allowed a sampling. The same friends maintained a regular production of home brew, cooled in a specially built wooden tank at the base of the windmill. These beverages, from my observation, were consumed in moderation, always with meals.

I cannot recall beer being served in our home, but there was evidence of my father's earlier activity in production home brew: bottles, caps, the bottle capper, and paper sacks filled with hops, which gave a pungent aroma to the attic room in which these things were stored. I believe that my father's approach to the consumption of alcohol was based on European standards of enjoyment and reasonable moderation. But I suspect that neither local option nor the Volstead Act were more than minor inconveniences which he was able to overcome when the need arose.

With the singing of Danish carols and the opening of gifts before a candle-decked tree, Christmas was celebrated on Christmas Eve rather than on Christmas Day. In an effort to avoid taking away from the religious nature of Christmas, the possibility of a real Santa Claus had been consciously dispelled from the beginning. This approach at least allowed the opening of gifts without having to wait to allow Santa to come down the chimney during the night.

I was the only child of immigrant parents in my class, probably, during the years I attended, in the entire school. I can't recall any feelings of discrimination, and I remember nothing but impartial treatment. But, at some point, I must have realized that my family's origin was a bit different, that the Pilgrim Fathers were not my forefathers, and that it was not my ancestors who Mr. Lincoln said had brought forth on this continent a new nation.

My childhood images of Danes and of things Danish were based on the first-generation Danes, relatives and others, whom I had encountered, on photographs of the relatives back in Denmark, on letters written in a strange hand, and on overheard reminiscences about the 'Old Country'. I saw old men, sometimes with stern faces, with large mustaches or side whiskers, dressed in black and with old-fashioned his shoes. I saw women with long dresses, their hair held in place with large hairpins. I heard a language, part of which I could understand, but one which would not have been understood at all by any of my friends. I heard English, when it was used, spoken often imperfectly and always with an accent. Totally unaware of my own provincialism and overlooking the affection and kindness of my relatives, I came to feel, without giving expression to my feelings, that most things Danish were old-fashioned and somehow backward. Curiously, I did not, beyond a degree usual for any child, see my mother in the same light; I was even unaware that she spoke with an accent until someone told me.

As I reflect on it, I am certain that as a child I had a strong determination not to be different from my peers, to be truly American, as I perceived them. I wanted to forget or ignore my Danish heritage; at least, I did not want evidence of it to be noticeable to my classmates and friends.

I have mentioned these things because they reflect my feelings at that time, and I suspect that others, under similar circumstances, have felt the same. I don't feel apologetic; I know that I gradually came to see these things in proper perspective and that I have a good feeling about my heritage.

Rolvaag, in *Giants in the Earth*, and its sequel, *Peder Victorious*, the story of the second generation, saw as a tragedy of the emigration that the child "slips into a world where his mother cannot go."[36] He felt that the second generation had to revolt against its elders to secure its place in American society. Rolvaag, of course, wrote of an earlier period, a period in which the contrasts between the generations were more sharply drawn. In any event, in my family, such emotions, to the extent that they may have existed, could hardly be described in words as strong as tragedy or revolt. And an interest in and an affection for our heritage has continued even in my children. But, in general, has the pressure for immigrants to become Americanized resulted in an undue loss of the earlier culture and tradition? I'm not sure.

Whatever the answer, it is difficult to dispute the conclusions of Gudrun Gvaale when she wrote the "The exchange of languages, the changing of cultures, the mixture of peoples, the whole process of

---

[36]Rolvaag, O.E. *Peder Victorious*. Harper and Row, New York. Perennial Classic edition, 1929. p vii.

184

Americanization moves inexorably without regard to who resists it, or what it costs, or what values are lost in (the) transformation."[37]

In the case of my parents, was the cost worthwhile? Did the reality live up to the promise? For them, more because of the freedom and opportunity they found than because of material gain, I would conclude:" Emphatically yes!"

As for me, the second generation American: I can't tell you how happy I am that they decided to come. I'm glad they got "West-fever". I'm happy to be here!

[37]Gvalle, Gudrun Hovde. *Ole Edvart Roelvaag: Nordmann og Amerika*. Oslo, 1962, PP. 372-385. (Introduction to ref 7., translated and adapted from the Norwegian by Einar Haugen.) xvi.

Epilogue, by Robert J. Thomsen

I can only hope that what you are holding in your hand does justice to Fred, Nina, Sophia, and John's efforts. These stories have, indeed, not found the incinerator. Here I will fill in some gaps about what Fred and Nina have already written beginning with the oldest of the Hansens.

Ole Hansen's father, **Hans Jensen** (1820-1881), was born near Slagelse, Denmark. This small city on the west coast of Zealand is at the eastern end of the bridge, which now spans the Store Bælt (Great Belt), the wide channel separating Zealand from Funen. Hans was the younger son of a small farm owner. He was confirmed in the Lutheran Church at about age 14; since he would not inherit the farm, he then was on his own to make a living. He worked for farmers for several years, married, and served the compulsory service in the Danish army. On his return he and his wife did subsistence farming near the town of Reersø, which is 17 miles north of Slagelse on a small peninsula jutting out into the Store Bælt. They had seven children, all sons.

Ole's mother, **Marie Jensdatter** (1821-1906), was born near Halbæk, Denmark in western Zealand, about thirty miles northwest from Slagelse. Orphaned early in life, she lived in foster care and after confirmation worked as a goose herder on a farm near Reersø. Except for catechism training she never went to school but taught herself how to read and write so that she could exchange letters with her husband in the army and later with her children and relations. She remained with Ole and his family near Hecla until her death in 1906.

The oldest of Ole's brothers, **Jens Peter Hansen,** emigrated alone at age 24 in about 1867 to Greenville, Michigan, a common destination for Danes. The rest of the family followed in 1870 when Hans was age 50, Marie 49, and the six younger sons 20, 18, 16, 14, 12, and 4. Those of age each got jobs in the Greenville lumber industry. By the time of father Hans' death in 1881, the older boys had already dispersed to other places. Jens Peter farmed in Michigan, Hans Peter farmed in northeast Wisconsin, Nils had a clothing store in Ashland, Wisconsin, and Lars Peter became a tailor in the Pacific Northwest.

Sophia's husband, **Ole Peter Hansen**, was born in 1857, the fifth of the seven sons. When Hans Jensen died in 1881 Ole, along with his younger brothers and his widowed mother, listened to the call of free fertile land and homesteaded in Dakota Territory.

Ole's next youngest brother, **Frederick Hansen,** was the namesake of our main author. Born in 1858, he stayed in South Dakota with Ole, George, and his mother for a time, but then married the daughter of a homesteader and farmed nearby. He died at age 30 on November 8, 1888.

Jørgen (George) Peter Hansen, the youngest, was born in 1865. George never married and remained with Ole and family near Hecla until his untimely death on July 30, 1888 from a lightning strike while working in the fields.

Sophia Thomsen Ganderup Hansen, Ole's wife and Fred's mother, was from southern Jutland in the border area between Denmark and Germany. When she was born in 1857 the area of Sleswig (that is the Danish spelling) was under the Danish crown, but in 1864 the Prussians under Otto von Bismarck waged a quick and decisive war culminating in the famous battle at Døbbel Mill on April 18, 1864. Denmark was forced to cede Sleswig to Prussia, including the area where Sophia and her family were living. Her home was Danish with Danish language, customs, food, and music, but outside the home she had to deal with the German language, administration, school, and culture.

Sophia was the ninth of eleven children; by the time Sophia was old enough to remember, five of her siblings were already out of the house. Of those at home the oldest, Niels, emigrated to Clinton,

Iowa, in 1872 where first he farmed and then set up a successful shoemaking and repair business in town. He probably sent letters home describing his life in America, as well as his marriage to a girl from Bevtoft, just twelve miles up the road from his hometown of Rødekro. They had two children, Marie and John N.

Sophia's immigration would be called by historians "chain immigration." She followed her older brother, and a year later her younger brother Jes (later known in America as John) followed her to Clinton. This was my grandfather. He figures prominently in some of these stories. **Jes Thomsen Ganderup** (in America **John Thomsen**) was born on October 19, 1862. As he approached age twenty, he was subject to the draft into the Prussian army. To avoid that, he emigrated to Clinton. Later he attended veterinary school in Toronto, Ontario, and in 1895 set up a practice in Armstrong, Iowa. His first wife, Bina, died in 1913. He married his second wife, Kirstine Thisgaard, in 1919, and on June 2, 1921 their only son, John G Thomsen, was born. This was my father. John died suddenly from a heart attack on October 8, 1923.

Sophia died at age 82 on June 14, 1943 during the darkest parts of World War II. She was doubtless very saddened by the reports of suffering in her native Denmark during the invasion and occupation by Nazi Germany and did not live to see its liberation.

Ole and Sophia married in 1887 and had three children: Olga, George, and Fred. The oldest was **Olga Sophia Hansen Litzenberg.** She was born on March 18, 1890, in a wooden frame farm house without electricity or indoor plumbing. She attended a one-room schoolhouse just one mile north of their home. Her formative years were spent on the farm where the needs of the family demanded she do her share of farm chores: driving horses, helping with field work, and caring for livestock. She grew up around farm animals of all kinds; she later said that she practiced animal dissection on mice in the granary.[38] After completion of eighth grade, she commuted by train fifty miles to the Aberdeen Normal School for three years of high school and then completed her final year of high school education at the new school in nearby Hecla.

Olga Hansen Litzenberg, M.D. – 1940's

Initially she wanted to become a veterinarian like her Uncle John in Armstrong, Iowa, just as her brother Fred was to become. Veterinary medicine was considered a man's profession and schools at that time did not admit women, so she enrolled in the University of Minnesota in the human medical school curriculum. She received her B.S. degree in 1913 and M.D. degree as the only woman in her class in 1915.

Olga remained affiliated with the University of Minnesota for her entire career in Internal Medicine. Her primary areas of expertise were cardiology and diabetes. She pioneered the use of a new instrument, the electrocardiogram, and in 1923 was the first in Minneapolis to treat a private patient with insulin for diabetic coma. Her publications included such diverse topics as "Magnesium Sulfate in Arsenic Poisoning," "Important Symptoms in Circulatory Disease," "Experimental Jaundice," and "Multiple Myeloma." She

---

[38] Minneapolis Tribune June 6, 1965.

held a teaching position at the University of Minnesota School of Medicine from 1917 to 1927 as director of the outpatient Cardiac Clinic.[39] In 1920 Olga joined the Nicollet Clinic, a group of University of Minnesota faculty members.

Another member of that clinic was obstetrician and gynecologist Jennings Crawford Litzenberg, whom Olga would later marry. Jennings was born in Iowa on April 6, 1870, to parents who could both trace their American lineage back at least five generations to precolonial roots. Jennings received his M.D. from the University of Minnesota in 1899 and soon turned his interests to the field of obstetrics.

In 1902 he married Elizabeth Fisher, and in a happy marriage they had two children. In 1910 he was appointed Associate Professor of Obstetrics and Gynecology, the first time that these two specialties were recognized as being combined. He was Professor and Head of the OB-Gyn department from 1913 to 1938. His beloved Elizabeth died in 1927. During the next seven years, the relationship between Jennings and Olga grew; initially student and mentor, it shifted to deep respect and love. When Olga was 41 she and Jennings were quietly married.

Especially at the beginning of Olga's career she was a woman in a man's world—the profession of medicine—but she did not let that get in her way. Her quiet self-confident competence spoke for itself throughout her career and her marriage. "I never felt victimized by male prejudice," she was quoted as saying. "In this work you don't think of yourself as a woman."[40] At work she remarked that she was a physician first and only happened to be a woman; she remained Dr. Olga Hansen in the clinic and hospital, but was Mrs. Litzenberg

---

[39] Personal file—application for membership in the Hennepin County Medical Society. In possession of Robert J. Thomsen.
[40] Minneapolis Tribune, June 14, 1970.

at home.[41] Her attitude was an inspiration to many generations of women medical students.[42]

Following Jennings' death on August 15, 1948, Olga continued her busy practice at the Nicollet Clinic until her retirement in 1970. Olga had no children of her own, but was proud of her adopted daughter, Jeanette Norris, and two step-children, Karl and Avis Litzenberg.

All of her life her family continued to be important to her, and no one more so than Fred. The bonds of siblings were iron tight. Her health gradually deteriorated from a series of strokes. Near the end of Olga's life, Fred and Nina convinced her to spend her last days with them in Independence, Missouri, where she died on August 10, 1975 at the age of 85.

Olga and Fred's middle brother was **George Niel Hansen.** Born November 17, 1892, George attended the University of Minnesota, concentrating in animal husbandry, a field in which he had developed some expertise through experience living on the farm. He died suddenly in 1918 at age 26, probably from sepsis from an infected sinus.

Frederic Wilhelm Hansen, Sr. and Nina Strahan Hansen are the authors of all but one of our stories. Fred was born on June 30, 1895, on the family farm south of Hecla. Nina was born on May 15, 1897, in Perry, Oklahoma Territory. Her father was a laborer who followed the work opportunities, and the family followed him. Stops included Yale and Bartlesville, Oklahoma; Wichita, Kansas; and, finally, Kansas City, Missouri. Nina was working in Kansas City in 1915 when she met a captivating young veterinary student on a blind date.

---

[41] Op cit.

[42] Profile of Dr. Olga Hansen Litzenberg by James A. Johnson—from private files.

On March 3, 1917, Fred and Nina were married by a Justice of the Peace. Fred finished his veterinary degree later in the spring and soon was inducted into the United States Army as a veterinarian caring for the Army's horses in Battle Creek, Michigan. Frederic W. Hansen, Jr. came along in December. After the end of WWI attempts to practice veterinary medicine in Wadena, Minneapolis, and Lakeville, Minnesota, proved to be unsuccessful for one reason or another, but in 1923 they located to a farm near Pelican Rapids, Minnesota, 200 miles to the northwest of Minneapolis. There they farmed, had a successful veterinary practice, and raised their son, Fred. Jr. When Fred Jr. returned from schooling with a new wife and his own veterinary degree, father and son practiced together.

Early in 1942, Fred Sr. and Nina moved to the Twin Cities, where Fred took an inspection job in the stock yards. At first, they lived on Carter Avenue in St. Paul with Fred's mother, Sophia, to take care of her in her final time of life. After Sophia's death in 1943, they moved to an apartment at Highland Village and Fred continued work at the stock yards.

Next came a move in 1948 to Denver, Colorado, for similar veterinary work. In March 1954, they moved again, this time to Wichita, Kansas, then back to Denver where Fred was in charge of the Federal Inspection at the stockyards. Meanwhile they purchased a home in Independence, Missouri, where the bulk of Nina's family lived. Fred retired on October 1, 1962, and soon began a successful retirement in Independence filled with many happy vacation trips.

Late in life they moved to Alexandria, Virginia, to be near Fred and Florence. There Fred Sr died on December 4, 1986, at age 89. He and Nina had been married for over 69 years. Nina lived almost ten more years and died April 11, 1996 just short of her 99th birthday. Both are buried at Arlington National Cemetery.

Nina and Fred Sr.'s only child was **Frederic W. Hansen, Jr.** He was born in Kansas City, Missouri, on December 12, 1917 and grew up in Pelican Rapids, Minnesota, first on the farm and then in town. Fred Jr.'s wife, **Florence Marie Logan Hansen,** also grew up in Pelican Rapids. She was born on May 15, 1919, in Fargo, North Dakota, of solid Norwegian heritage. The family soon moved back to Pelican Rapids where Fred and Florence were high school sweethearts.

After Fred graduated from high school, he did some preparatory studies at North Dakota State College in Fargo and then enrolled in Veterinary College at the University of Kansas in Manhattan in the fall of 1936. Fred and Florence were married on July 29, 1938 in Branson, Missouri, and in the autumn they went back to Manhattan for Fred Jr.'s last year of veterinary school. After graduation they returned to Pelican Rapids, where father and son practiced together before Fred Sr.'s move to Minneapolis.

They remained in Pelican Rapids while Fred Jr. practiced veterinary medicine and they began a family. In April of 1941 their first daughter was born, followed by their second in December 1943. Fred, Jr. served in the United States Army during WWII from April 1943 to May, 1946. Their third daughter came along in August 1948. November 1950 began a series of moves to take various positions in veterinary medicine, including Fort Morgan, Colorado; Oklahoma City; Montpelier, Vermont; Oklahoma City again; and finally Washington, D.C. On retirement they lived in Springfield, Virginia. Florence died on July 10, 2001, in Springfield and Fred Jr. died just eight days later, on July 18, 2001. Both are buried at Arlington National Cemetery.

John G. Thomsen was born on June 2, 1921 and grew up in Armstrong, Iowa. His father, John Thomsen, died when John G. was just two years old. John G. went to St. Olaf College and then to medical school at the University of Iowa. He specialized in dermatology and practiced in Des Moines until retirement. He died on December 19, 1998 and his ashes are interred next to the graves of his parents in Ringsted, Iowa.

Acknowledgements
by Robert J. Thomsen

First, I am deeply grateful that Fred, Nina, and Sophia each took the trouble to preserve these memories of their lives. Their examples serve as an inspiration to all of us to do the same for our future generations. Our stories, humble or grand, deserve to be preserved as our legacy.

I am also grateful to my newly found cousins, Sharry, Claudia, and AnnMarie; I call them the Hansen cousins, even though each has long since through marriage shed the Hansen surname. It has been a delight to work with them in making this little book.

I thank my wife, Michelle, and my son, Davis, for proofreading and making valuable suggestions on both form and content.

About the Author

Robert J. Thomsen is a retired dermatologist who has embraced writing as his new vocation. His past published works have included a book of poetry about dermatologists and a book co-authored with Eugene N. Kovalenko about understanding dreams. His current writing projects include an extensive biography of his grandfather, John Thomsen, his own memoirs, and a history of Boy Scouts in Los Alamos, New Mexico. He lives with his wife of over fifty years, Michelle, dividing time between Rochester, Minnesota and the family cabin near Bigfork, Minnesota.

He would love to hear any comments about the stories in *Lucky Grandpa Had a Horse* or any issues raised by it. Please check out his website www.robertjthomsen.com.

www.ingramcontent.com/pod-product-compliance
Lightning Source LLC
Chambersburg PA
CBHW051308120626
46547CB00015B/2139